SKINNER'S PHILOSOPHY

Paul T. Sagal

UNIVERSITY
PRESS OF
AMERICA

Copyright © 1981 by

University Press of America, Inc.™

P.O. Box 19101, Washington, DC 20036

Library of Congress Cataloging in Publication Data

Sagal, Paul T
   Skinner's philosophy.

   Bibliography: p.
   1. Skinner, Burrhus Frederic, 1904-   . 2. Psy-
chology--Philosophy. 3. Behaviorism (Psychology)
4. Skinner, Burrhus Frederic, 1904-   . Beyond freedom
and dignity. I. Title.
BF38.S216   150.19'434   80-5737
ISBN 0-8191-1432-4
ISBN 0-8191-1433-2 (pbk.)

SKINNER'S PHILOSOPHY

TABLE OF CONTENTS

ACKNOWLEDGEMENTS

Acknowledgments for permission to reprint material are made to the following:

From "Phylogeny and Ontogeny of Behavior," Skinner, B. F., _Science_, Vol. 153 pp. 1205-1213, 9 Sept. 1966. Copyright 1966 by the American Association for the Advancement of Science.

From "Behaviorism at Fifty," Skinner, B. F., _Science_, Vol. 140 pp. 951-958, 31 May 1963. Copyright 1963 by the American Association for the Advancement of Science.

From "The Inside Story," Skinner, B. F. reprinted from _Psychology Today_, copyright 1969, Ziff-Davis Publishing Company.

From _Beyond Freedom and Dignity_, Skinner, B. F. Copyright 1971, Alfred A. Knopf Inc.

From _Science and Human Behavior_, Skinner, B. F. Copyright 1953, MacMillan Publishing Co., Inc.

From _Language and Philosophy_ edited by Sidney Hook. Copyright 1969 by New York University (New York University Press).

From _Ontological Relativity and Other Essays_, Quine, W. V. O. Copyright 1969, Columbia University Press.

PREFACE

Any book, even as modest an effort as
Skinner's Philosophy, owes much to many people.
All the contributors to my history of conditioning, in this respect, are too numerous to mention.
I am happy to single out Judson and Ilona Webb who
introduced me to Skinner's work, and Socorro
Prieto who did her usual excellent job typing the
manuscript. I would like to thank my family,
Karen, Chip, Jared, Lanny, Sandy, Lil and my
mother for being family. The book is dedicated to
the memories of my father-in-law, William Gold,
and especially my father, Joseph Sagal.

INTRODUCTION

The ideas of B. F. Skinner are widely publicized, much maligned, and little understood. Skinner is one of the two or three most influential professional psychologists of this century. He is also a popular philosopher; that is to say, his philosophy is almost completely ignored by professional philosophers. Professional psychologists, on the other hand, not only ignore his philosophy but are embarrassed by Skinner's speculative bent. Skinner's philosophy then, tends to get a wide but hardly a fair hearing. The present book aims at providing Skinner with that fair hearing. Unlike Skinner himself, we think that a reader cannot simply plunge into Beyond Freedom and Dignity, and adequately understand just what is going on. Such a plunge is apt to produce nothing more than multifarious gut reactions. Some like it, most do not. Much of Skinner's Philosophy serves as prolegomena--as introduction--to Beyond Freedom and Dignity.

In this work, Skinner's system of psychology and his theory of science are given a reasonably thorough airing in a critical manner. The prospective reader of Beyond Freedom and Dignity should get to know Skinner the scientist--Skinner the theoretician. Some applications of Skinner's work are also discussed. The reader should view some of the fruits of Skinner's work. And finally the reader should confront Beyond Freedom and Dignity and see how the broad strokes of Skinnerian philosophy mix with Skinnerian science. The mix, we contend, does not form a compound. Like oil and water, Skinner's philosophy and his science do not form a unity, they just go their separate ways; they are immiscible. Yet Skinner emphatically sees his own work as a unity, and unless the reader attempts to approach Skinner's work as Skinner himself does, he is likely to come away with but a superficial understanding. Our study concludes with an examination of psychology as a philosophic

method. We are confronted with epistemology
(theory of knowledge) psychologized (or more spe-
cifically--epistemology Skinnerized). Here too,
Skinner's sin lies in pushing a good thing too far.
Psychology, even <u>good psychology</u>, can never be
pushed far enough to become an adequate total philosophy. The author confesses in advance to a
sympathy for Skinner's science, and an antipathy
for some of his politics.

CHAPTER I

Skinner and the Enlightenment Ideal

Skinner is in many ways a man of the enlightenment--a throwback to that age dominated by faith in science and the perfectibility of man. Our age is a much more sceptical one. We see our 18th Century brethren as a bit utopian, even simpleminded. We have seen tremendous scientific and technological progress, yet we have also seen world wars and decreased quality of life. We have come to a new understanding of science itself. We pride ourselves on being much more sophisticated than those enlightenment optimists. Skinner might well say that the only thing wrong with the faith of the enlightenment was that it was premature, especially in respect to its knowledge of, and hopes for, man.

Many set out to do for psychology, for human nature, what Sir Isaac Newton did for nature itself. Newton unlocked the door to nature's secrets. A number of things about Newton's achievement need to be stressed. Newton managed to bring together and explain all natural phenomena without appealing to prima facie non-physical, metaphysical, or theological causes. In fact, the very notion of cause was somewhat subtly redefined. Causes were no longer seen as things behind nature--active agencies, powers, real essences. The causes were the natural phenomena themselves. When we can show a lawful relation between two sorts of events, then and only then may we term one event the cause of the other. In mathematical language cause enters the picture when we deal with functions. The principle of causality, or the uniformity of nature, can then be put as follows: Uniform values to independent variables yield uniform values for dependent variables.

The fact that Newton's work was recognized for the contribution it was reflected an appreciation of the distinction between genuine and bogus

1

explanation. It was not merely that Newtonian science worked, but that it was free of extra-physical notions. Theology or metaphysics, if not completely absent from Newton's scheme, were kept well in the background. We can make this clear by being a bit more specific. The great unifying principle of Newtonian physics was the law of universal gravitation. It can be stated thus: $F = \dfrac{gM_1 \times M_2}{r^2}$ where F is a force, M_1 and M_2 are masses, g the gravitational constant, and r^2 the square of the distance between the two masses. The language of Newtonian physics was preëminently the language of force, mass and distance. One needed geometry to measure distance, rational mechanics for mass and Newtonian dynamics for force--but nowhere did one need the Bible, or scholastic or more modern metaphysics. The autonomy of physics was reflected in an obvious way in Newtonian physics. Furthermore, laws like universal gravitation were subject to empirical test. One had the sense of responding rather than dictating to nature. When it came to explaining just what the force of universal gravitation was--just how the mechanism of 'attraction' worked--Newton resisted the temptation to speculate. Not to have done so would obviously have been to go beyond physics. At such a point the notion would no longer have been tied to lawful relations among phenomena. One would have had to get behind the phenomena. Newton wished to avoid hypotheses-- hypotheses non fingo. More accurately, what he avoided for the most part was a certain kind of speculation--speculation which involved going behind the phenomena which were explained by physical laws like universal gravitation.

If we wanted to introduce the term theory at this point, we could say that Newton's work was clearly theoretical in the following sense: he employed terms which were abstract compared to the terms of everyday life. It is in some sense a theoretical achievement to come up with working notions of distance, mass and force. (Newton was, of course, building on the work of others in this

2

area.) Newton was able to frame putative laws which were subject to empirical test. He certainly went beyond the facts at hand. If theorizing involves extrapolation and interpolation, then Newton was most assuredly a theoretician. Yet Newton's work was not theoretical in the following sense: he did not attempt to explain the laws he came up with (laws relating physical phenomena) through appeal to events, entities, or laws governing these entities at some extra-physical level. No appeal to explanation by means of the mechanism within or the divinity without was made. This kind of theoretical speculation Newton resisted.

The enlightenment was in a very real sense the light reflected, refracted and dispersed by Newton's work. "God said, let there be Newton, and there was light." It was natural, then, for thinkers to attempt to apply Newton to human nature. This was not the first time that work in physics led directly to the study of man. One could speak in general of applying the study of physical nature to the study of human nature, but the basic questions concerned the precise character of the application. Were we, for instance, simply to apply the method of physics to the study of man, were we in some sense to derive laws governing human nature from the laws of physics, or were we simply to employ the language of physics in our psychological and anthropological investigations? In the 17th Century, Thomas Hobbes attempted to build a psychology upon the foundations of Galilean mechanics. Hobbes, it seems clear, sought something like a reduction of psychology to physics, to the principles governing matter and motion.

> For seeing life is but a motion of limbs, the beginning whereof is in some principal part within; why may not we say, that all automata (engines that move themselves by springs and wheels as doth a watch) have an artificial life. For what

3

is the _heart_, but a _spring_; and the
nerves, but so many springs; and the
joints but so many _wheels_, giving motion
to the whole body, such as was intended
by the artificer.[1]

There were any number of attempts to 'apply'
Newton to human nature during the 18th Century.
These ranged from the materialism of La Mettrie and
de Holbach to the sensationalism of Condillac. But
the Newtonian spirit is perhaps best captured,
surprisingly enough, in the early sections of David
Hume's _A Treatise of Human Nature_. This is surprising because Hume's work is known chiefly for
its sceptical conclusions, conclusions which
threatened Newtonian science itself. Still, it is
clear that the young Hume saw himself as following
in Newton's footsteps. Hume was after a science of
human nature. He looked at such a science as being
even more fundamental than physics, for it dealt
with the subject--the Knower--and its results would
be useful to all sciences. It was in a sense a
science of science. Its task was to explain _how_
we know--the other sciences all dealt with _what_ we
know.

Newton's principle of universal gravitation is
neatly paralleled by Hume's principle of the
association of ideas. The force of association
among ideas is the universal force in human nature.
This constructive or systematic aspect of Hume's
philosophy comes out clearly in the following:

There are, therefore, the principles
of union or cohesion among our simple
ideas, and in the imagination supply
the place of that inseparable connection, by which they are united in our
memory. Here is a kind of _attraction_,
which in the mental world will be found
to have as extraordinary effects as in
the natural, and to show itself in as

[1]Thomas Hobbes, _Leviathan_ (Introduction).

many and as various forms. Its effects
are everywhere conspicuous; but as to
its causes they are mostly unknown, and
must be resolved into <u>original</u> qualities
of human nature, which I do not pretend
to explain. Nothing is more requisite
for a true philosopher, than to restrain
the intemperate desire of searching into
causes; and having established any
doctrine upon a sufficient number of
experiments, rest contented with that
when he sees a further examination would
lead him into obscure and uncertain
speculations. In that case his inquiry
would be much better employed in examin-
ing the effects than the causes of his
principle.[2]

Here we find Hume following Newton's rules of
philosophizing. Hume no more seeks to explain the
mechanics of association than Newton does gravitation. Clearly, when Hume set out to write his
treatise, he thought of himself as doing experimental science. The world he was investigating
was the world of simple perceptions, just as
Newtonian science investigated material points,
simple material bodies.

But the science of human nature, the science
which was supposed to be even more useful to man
than Newton's science, never really got off the
ground. In Hume's treatise, a science of human
nature seemed to lead inevitably to a scepticism
which called into question all science. In general,
nothing in the 18th Century came close to doing for
man what Newton did for nature. But why? Any number of answers come to mind: Man is just not the
kind of thing that can be treated in a scientific
way. Man is just a little lower than the angels,
and he is enough of a spiritual being to require
super or extra-scientific treatment. Nature might
not have purposes or goals in the way Aristotle

_____

[2]David Hume, <u>A</u> <u>Treatise</u> <u>of</u> <u>Human</u> <u>Nature</u>, (I,
I, 4).

thought, but man certainly does. Explanation of
human action which neglects the whys and wherefores
was unacceptable even to Plato's Socrates. This
line of argument, or something like it, may be
labeled reactionary, because it sought to go back
to some pre-enlightenment, pre-scientific view of
man. Souls were perhaps banished from physical
nature by Galileo and Newton, but there was still
a place for them in man. The philosophical-
theological approach to physical nature had to give
way to the scientific, yet it still held sway with
regard to man.

But the reactionary position, though comfort-
ing to many, was hardly entailed by the failure of
18th Century science to come up with a science of
human nature. When we look more closely, we see
that what was wrong with 18th Century science of
man was that it was bad science--and not that it
was good science failing because of the nature of
the subject matter. The Newtonian model was so
powerful that the temptation to take it over lock,
stock and barrel was too powerful to resist. One
or the other of two moves were made. (1) Man is
nothing but a machine (The Hobbesian move), therefore, we should be able to explain human behavior
in terms of and by principles belonging to physics.
But this approach, though having   simplicity on
its side, was hardly plausible. As Hobbes well
knew, this approach--call it materialism--had to
reduce all human thought and action to physical
motions. One can only say that thinking about
tomorrow's picnic and writing a letter to a friend
seem to involve more than physical motions.

That a reduction of thought and action is
possible or plausible is a task for the materialist
psychologist to demonstrate. He has a program.
The regularities of human thought and action are to
be described in terms of, and derived as, theorems
from principles of physics. We are still waiting
for contemporary materialists, with all the results
of modern neuro-physiology at their fingertips, to
come up with a semblance of such a reduction.

6

Obviously, the materialist psychology of the enlightenment was grossly premature. (2) The other approach taken by scientists of human nature, we might term dualistic. Its roots were in Descartes, but it was most clearly expressed in John Locke's new way of ideas and in subsequent British empiricism (like Hume's). The dualistic psychologist does not seek a reduction of psychology to physics, but rather an autonomous science of psychology quite strictly analogous to the science of physics. Corresponding to the material world with its point masses--its simple material bodies--is the mental world with its simple ideas or perceptions. The psychologist looks for laws governing the behavior of these simple mental entities in much the same way as the physicist looks for laws governing the behavior of the simple material entities. It is, of course, in this context that we see the point of the pretended analogy between universal gravitation and association of ideas. But the plausibility of the dualistic line depends upon our taking quite seriously the notion of a mental world with mental elements--psychological atomism, if you will. This is not an easy thing to do. Locke and his comrades claimed that we could directly introspect these entities. The author cannot, but one might argue that the point masses (the simple material bodies) are not themselves subject to observation. They are rather abstractions made from the complex material bodies we are familiar with in everyday life, i.e., chairs, tables, etc. But in this case the material from which abstraction or idealization is made is familiar and publicly observable. This does not seem to be the case with psychological atomism. At best the psychological atoms are abstractions from what is sometimes termed "the stream of experience." And this stream of experience is itself not a publicly observable phenomena. Physics was able to progress very considerably because of the possibility of public, objective, experimental test procedure. In dualistic psychology this was impossible. The empirical aspect of physics (and, of course, we all want to be empiricists), comes into play with experiment and testimony. It was claimed that this dualistic psychology was based on experience (was empirical), but experience here was a private matter, and therefore could not employ the methods which had worked so well in natural science. In this way the analogy with physics, which was so important to psychological atomism, had to break down. For even if the ontological part of the analogy--the analogy between the physical world and the mental world--was accepted, the mental world could not admit of the method of experiment and test which played such a major role in physical science.

Where are we then? We have to rule out the Scylla of materialist reductionism and the Charybdis of psychological dualism. But these do not exhaust the possibilities for a science of human nature. This enlightenment dream needn't be cast aside with the de facto failure of enlightenment thought. It just seems to be the case that the Newton of human nature cannot be, or could not have been, a materialist reductionist or a psychological dualist.

Perhaps we can learn something from the failures of our two enlightenment approaches. Materialism remained merely a vague promise because of its commitment to reduction. Its strong point was its simplicity--its emphasis upon the continuity between physics and psychology--on there being a single world populated by physical objects. It is precisely here where materialism was strongest that psychological atomism was weakest. It avoided the pitfalls of reductionism by preserving the autonomy of psychology but at the price of bifurcating reality--dividing it up into two realms. Now the interaction problem--the problem of trans-world communication--has long troubled philosophers and psychologists, but it seems the more fundamental problem lies with the mental world itself. Is the notion of such a world itself intelligible, much less useful? There is room, of course, for much argument here. To avoid at least some of the argument, let us simply suppose _ceteris paribus_ it would be better for a science of human nature to eschew the notion of a _mental world_.

Putting our comments about materialism and dualism along side one another, what do we come up with as _desiderata_ for a science of psychology? We seek a psychology which will be materialistic in the sense of being involved exclusively with those entities which physics or natural science is involved and which will be _autonomous_ in the sense that it will not treat the _principles_ of psychology as corollaries to the principles of physics. This involves _anti-_ or perhaps simply _non-reductionism_. Psychology is not to be deduced from physics. It is in this guise that the enlightenment dream lives. In the twentieth century the dream shines brightest perhaps in the work of John Dewey and B. F. Skinner.

CHAPTER II

Dewey, Watson and Thorndike

John Dewey considered his own study of human
nature to be squarely in the Humean tradition.
Dewey, of course, emphasized the constructive
rather than the sceptical role of Hume's teaching.
Hume's

> constructive idea is that a knowledge of
> human nature provides a map or chart of
> all humane and social subjects, and that
> with this chart in our possession we can
> find our way intelligently about through
> all the complexities of the phenomena of
> economics, politics, religious beliefs,
> etc. Indeed, he went further, and held
> that human nature gives also the key to
> the science of the physical world, since
> when all is said and done they are also
> the products of the workings of the human
> mind. It is likely that in enthusiasm
> for a new idea, Hume carried it too far.
> But there is to my mind an inexpugnable
> element of truth in his teaching. Human
> nature is at least a contributing factor
> to the _form_ which even natural science
> takes, although it may not give the key
> to its _content_ in the degree which Hume
> supposed.[3]

Dewey saw the importance of a science of human
nature, but he never attempted to develop one in
any systematic manner. The closest he came was his
Human Nature and Conduct from which we quoted
above. Dewey did, however, contribute a very
important paper in the foundations of psychology
which does have direct bearing on our story. The

---

[3]John Dewey, Human Nature and Conduct, Modern
Library, Foreward, p. vi.

year was 1896 and the paper was On The Reflex Arc
Concept in Psychology.[4] The reflex arc theory
appears to fit our desiderata of a materialistic
(physicalistic) but non-reductionist psychology.
The arc is viewed as comprising three elements
or atoms: the stimulus, the response, and the
intermediary neuro-physiological link. The task of
psychology on this account would be the identification and description of reflex arcs. The working
assumption, of course, is that all human behavior
can be characterized in terms of reflex-arcs.
There is no attempt to deduce the existence of
reflex arcs from the principles of physics, and
still there is no overt attempt to introduce something non-physical into the picture. The brunt of
Dewey's criticism is directed at the elementarism
of the approach--the conception of the reflex arc
as composed of three separable and separate elements. The eighteenth century psychological
theories, whether materialistic or dualistic, were
all atomistic theories. This was in direct imita-
tion of the dominant physical picture of the day.
It is this atomism which Dewey finds unacceptable
in any form. (It, of course, did not carry the day
in physics either. But that is a different story.)
Dewey even found the reflex arc theory to contain
echoes of some older dualisms.

> The older dualism between sensation and
> idea is repeated in the current dualism
> of peripheral and central structures and
> functions; the older dualism of body and
> soul finds a distinct echo in the current
> dualism of stimulus and response. Instead
> of interpreting the character of sensation,
> idea and action from their place and func-
> tion in the sensorimotor circuit, we still
> incline to interpret the latter from our
> preconceived and preformulated ideas of

---

[4]John Dewey, "On the Reflex Arc Concept in
Psychology," The Psychological Review, 1896, reprinted in J. Ratner's "Dewey's Philosophy, Psychology and Scientific Method."

rigid distinctions between sensations, thoughts, and acts. The sensory stimulus is one thing, the central activity, standing for the idea, is another thing, and the motor discharge, standing for the act proper, is a third thing. As a result, the reflex arc is not a comprehensive or organic unity, but a patchwork of disjointed parts, a mechanical conjunction of unallied processes. What is needed is that the principle underlying the idea of the reflex arc as the fundamental psychical unity shall react into and determine the values of its constitutive factors.[5]

For Dewey, human behavior, human action, human conduct cannot be treated as a mechanical sequence or conjunction of unallied processes. A human act is an organic unity. And it is this organic unity which should serve as the unifying principle and controlling working hypothesis in psychology. Stimulus and response can only be identified by the functions they serve in a more comprehensive unity.

Dewey chooses the term co-ordination for this unity (though sometimes this term is reserved for the physiological side of this reality). Human action is more than a conjunction of physical movements. The more is not a matter of supplementing the conjunction of physical movements with something non-physical or psychical--the more concerns the organic unity, the purposeful nature of human behavior. But purposes are not themselves new atoms supplementing the original atoms of physical movements. Human behavior is purposeful because the consequences of action modify action. Man does what he does because of the consequences which have followed similar behavior in the past. This kind of consideration is completely absent from the reflex-arc account. Dewey uses the example of

---

[5]Ibid.

a child reaching for a candleflame. On the reflex-
arc account, the light or sensation of light serves
as stimulus for the grasping response; the result-
ant burn is in turn a stimulus to withdrawing the
hand. On Dewey's account the story can be told in
terms of a single coordination! And note how the
coordination incorporates the consequences of
behavior. The coordination is seeing-of-a-light-
that-means-pain-when-contact-occurs. Past consequences enter importantly.

Some of the above may perhaps be difficult to
follow. Dewey is not noted for his lucidity. We
are principally interested in Dewey's evaluation
of the reflex-arc idea. "The result is that the
reflex arc idea leaves us with a disjointed psychology, whether viewed from the standpoint of
development in the individual or in the race, or
that of the analysis of the mature consciousness."
It reflects a

> failure to see that the arc of which it
> is virtually a circuit, is a continual
> reconstruction, it breaks continuity and
> leaves us nothing but a series of jerks,
> the origin of each jerk to be sought out-
> side the process of experience itself, in
> either an external pressure of 'environ-
> ment', or else in an unaccountable
> spontaneous variation from within the
> 'soul' or the 'organism'.

It also fails

> to see the unity of activity, no matter
> how much it may part of unity, it still
> leaves us with sensation or peripheral
> stimulus idea, or central process (the
> equivalent of attention); and motor
> response, or act, as three disconnected
> existences, having to be somehow adjusted

14

to each other, whether through the
intervention of an extra-experimental
soul, or by mechanical push and pull.[6]

Dewey does not give us a precise explication
of terms, experimental results, or psychological
laws. The reflex arc paper was important as a
critique of elementarism, as an argument against
attempts to treat human action without coming to
grips with notions like purpose, intention, and
meaning. Of course, the challenge is to handle
these notions without de-physicalizing psychology.
Non-physical purposes and intentions would mark the
death of a physical science of psychology. Psychology would then have the unenviable task of
explaining how non-physical entities interact with
the physical world and serve as contributory causes
of human behavior. This would take us back to
Descartes and metaphysical psychology. The challenge to psychology (certainly implicit in Dewey's
paper), is to provide an explanation of human
action without appealing to entities inaccessible
to physical science and without destroying the
unity of human action by treating it as an unintel-
ligible conglomerate of artificially isolated elements. Dewey's own theory of coordination is perhaps a step in the right direction, but it is not
clear enough to permit responsible judgment.
Coordinations seem to involve both neurophysiological occurrences and overt behavior, but the
relation between the two sorts of phenomena is
hardly indicated.

Dewey's Reflex-Arc paper refuted a theory of
human behavior which did not come to be formulated
in any detail until 1913. The theory is Watsonian
Behaviorism. John Watson's goal was an objective
science of human behavior. He formulated a view of
the proper subject matter of psychology; psychology
could not be scientific unless it possessed a subject matter which would permit it to be scientific.

----

[6] Ibid., p. 360.

15

Not the realm of the mind, not consciousness, not thought or sensation, but what man does, behavior, is the proper subject matter of psychology. Furthermore, it is this subject matter which gives psychology autonomous status. The science of behavior has its own basic conceptions and principles. Its laws are not simply corrollaries to the principles of physics.

This much is certainly in line with our desiderata for a science of psychology. But does Watsonian behaviorism meet what might be termed "the Deweyan challenge?" Does it recognize the organic unity of human action? Does it avoid elementarism? What does Watson mean by "behavior?" Alas for Watson, behavior is just a matter of the movements of muscles. The realm of the mind is out, but in its place are only muscle-movements. It turns out that Watsonian behaviorism is not very different in its basics from the reflex-arc-theory. All behavior is a matter of reflexes, learned or unlearned. Learning is a matter of classical conditioning.[7] In an unlearned reflex, a stimulus-like a blow on the knee elicits a response--the raising of the knee. Learning or conditioning is a matter of associating another stimulus, say a drum-roll, with the original stimulus in such a way as eventually to permit the new stimulus to elicit the old response. All learning is exclusively a matter of keying old responses to new stimuli. All human action is to be built up from these simple reflexes--learned and unlearned. It is the reflex arc theory with the central or neurophysiological phase rubbed out. We needn't go into the details of Watson's theory. He never worked out the reduction of human actions to the sequences of reflexes; it remained a promise.

This is the first time we have dealt with a particular brand of behaviorism. To identify

---

[7]The theory of classical conditioning is the contribution of the Russian physiologist-psychologist, Ivan Pavlov.

behaviorism with Watson's variety is about as
reasonable as identifying materialism with the
theories of Democritus and Leucippus. Watson
popularized the term, was passionately devoted to
making psychology scientific, but was for the most
part more prophet and publicist than scientist.
Watsonian behaviorism was scientifically an anach-
ronism. However, he left psychology the fundamental task of finding an adequate behaviorism. It
was fortunate that psychology had Watson to kick
around.

Certainly, it is true that some human behavior
is a matter of reflex. But Watson's fault, though
a fault not original to him, was the reduction of
all human behavior to this reflex kind. A view of
behavior which supplements Watson's in an important
way is that of E. M. Thorndike. Put simply, what
we do, according to Thorndike, is largely a matter
of what has succeeded in the past. We learn by
trial and error. It is the consequences of
behavior which strengthen some behaviors and weaken
others. This is summed up in Thorndike's famous
law of effect. If a stimulus-response connection
is followed by a satisfier or reinforcer, then the
connection is strengthened; if followed by an
'annoyer' or aversive stimulus, the connection is
weakened. The key notions are satisfier and
annoyer--which bring back into psychology the
notions of pleasure and pain. Pleasure and pain
are, however, not defined subjectively.

By a satisfying state of affairs is meant
one which the animal does nothing to
avoid, often doing things which maintain
or renew it. By an annoying state of
affairs is meant one which the animal does
nothing to preserve, often doing things
which put an end to it.[8]

---

[8]E. L. Thorndike, The Elements of Psychology,
1913, p. 2.

Here purpose enters the picture through the emphasis upon consequences of behavior. But Thorndike
is certainly not a systematic theorist and does
not elaborate on his law of effect.

Watson studied rats; Thorndike studied cats.
Where did man enter the picture? Man was just
another animal. The working assumption for both
was that man's behavior was just more complex
than, and not different in kind from, the behavior
of other animals reasonably high up the phylo-
genetic scale. This emphasis on continuity was
largely a consequence of Darwinian biology. If
there was a break in the continuity of nature, it
seemed that life and not human life was that break.
Ultimately, language and culture set man apart.
But even these seem tied to certain biological
capabilities. The ultimate challenge for this
animal-centered psychology would be to provide an
account of language learning which would involve
methods and concepts themselves continuous with
studies in animal behavior. This will be described
in more detail later. There is a reductionist
flavor to this animal-centered psychology. The
working assumption is that a theory of human
behavior can be framed exclusively in terms of and
deduced from the principles of animal psychology.
But this brand of reduction has at least Darwin
and some hard experimental results in animal psychology going for it. It certainly is a less
ambitious kind of reduction than the reduction of
human behavior to the principles of matter and
motion.

In 1927, Bertrand Russell published a book
with the simple title Philosophy. The book put
forth a challenge--a challenge to psychology in
general and to behavioristic psychology in particular, to provide an adequate philosophical theory
of knowledge. In Philosophy, Russell pushes the
behaviorism of his day--largely that of Watson and
Thorndike--as far as it will go. Russell concludes that it does not go far enough. It needs
to be supplemented with more traditional

philosophical methods. The <u>objective</u> approach of behaviorism needs to be supplemented with the <u>subjective</u> or <u>introspective</u> approach of traditional philosophy and psychology.

> We decided contrary to the view of the behaviorists, that there are important facts which cannot be known except when the observer and the observed are the same person. The datum in perception, we decided is a private fact which can only be known directly to the percipient.[9]

Russell gave up behaviorism somewhat grudgingly, for he viewed philosophy as a discipline quite continuous with science. Philosophy was simply "more general" and "more critical." Now if there is more to man than a behaviorist science of psychology can get at, this is a serious indictment indeed of behaviorism. We cannot go into Russell's arguments, but it is clear that the heart of Russell's quarrel with behaviorism is over <u>perception</u>. And it is certainly true that (i) perception has always dominated philosophical inquiries into psychological problems and (ii) perception is perhaps the single most difficult problem to handle behavioristically. Other approaches to psychology almost have the study of perception as their <u>reason for being</u> (e.g., Gestalt Psychology). It <u>is</u> fair to say that the adequacy of behaviorism as a total psychology will stand or fall with its treatment of perception. Still, Russell's attempt to take behaviorism seriously was an important intellectual landmark. Among the chapters in the book <u>Philosophy</u> is "The Process of Learning in Animals and Infants." Russell strongly defends his concern with this kind of subject.

---

[9]Bertrand Russell, <u>An Outline of Philosophy</u> (original title: <u>Philosophy</u>), Meridian, 1960, p. 306.

The matters with which we shall be
concerned in this chapter belong to
behaviorist psychology, and in part to
pure physiology. Nevertheless, these
seem to me vital to a proper understanding of philosophy, since they are necessary
for an objective study of knowledge and
inference.[10]

In dealing with Watson and Thorndike, Russell
contributes some valuable conceptual clarification.
We have already indicated the subjective flavor of
pleasure and pain in Thorndike's own statement of
the Law of Effect. Thorndike's way out was also
presented. Russell takes a somewhat different
tact. He stresses the notion of effect. Really,
what the law amounts to is the fact that there are
situations in which an animal tends to repeat acts
which have led to them. Or in other words, certain
consequences increase the probability of behavior.
Or still more generally, consequences are important
for behavior. This is in no way to imply that the
future can determine the past. It is simply that
consequences of past instances of a certain form
of behavior will determine under what future circumstances future instances of the behavior will
be forthcoming. Watson is taken to task for hold-
ing that all learning can be reduced to the formula
of the conditioned reflex. Watson must be supplemented with Thorndike.

Dr. Watson considers one principle alone
sufficient to account for all animal and
human learning, namely the principle of
'learned reactions'. This principle may
be stated as follows: When the body of an
animal or human being has been exposed
sufficiently often to two roughly simul-
taneous stimuli, the earlier of them alone
tends to call out the response previously
called out by the other. Although I do

---

[10]Ibid., p. 33.

20

not agree with Dr. Watson in thinking
this principle alone sufficient, I do
agree that it is a principle of very great
importance. It is the modern form of the
principle of 'association'. The 'association of ideas' has played a great part in
philosophy, particularly in British philosophy. But it now appears that this is a
consequence of a wider and more primitive
principle, namely the association of
bodily processes.[11]

Russell attempts to treat language and perception by means of Watson-Thorndike. Language is
treated as a complex bodily habit, and Russell is
on the whole happy with the behaviorist account.
As we have indicated, things are otherwise with
perception. This is behaviorism's bête noire.

From the objective point of view, perception
is simply a species of sensitivity. What troubles
Russell is the difference between the way we know
the perceptions of others and the way we know our
own perceptions.

This is one of the weak spots in the
attempt at a philosophy from an objective standpoint. Such a philosophy
really assumed knowledge as a going concern, and takes for granted the world
which a man derives from his own perceptions. We cannot tackle all our philosophical problems by the objective method,
but it is worthwhile to proceed with it
as far as it will take us.[12]

Bertrand Russell's challenge was in an important way B. F. Skinner's stimulus to inquiry. A
successful response to the challenge would have to
come in two parts (i) a general systematic

---

[11]Ibid., p. 36.

[12]Ibid., p. 70.

presentation of the behaviorist position. Russell, as we saw, worked with a composite of Watson and Thorndike. (ii) An adequate treatment of perception--a treatment which would have to find some place for the facts of privacy, for the subjective-introspective approach <u>within</u> the broader framework of an objective psychology. This was a tall order, indeed.

Skinner encountered Russell's views on psychology in a series of articles Russell wrote in the mid-20's for the <u>Dial Magazine</u> as well as in <u>Philosophy</u>. Skinner at the time was just at the point of entering Harvard to do graduate work in psychology. There were significant influences on Skinner's attitude towards psychology which pre- and post-dated Russell's.[13] This was especially the case in connection with the details of experimental method and Skinner's general conception of science. But what Skinner got from Russell was a glimpse of behavioristic psychology as a philosophy--particularly as a total philosophy of man. Russell rejected this behaviorist philosophy, but only after an honest attempt to give it its due. To Skinner, Russell's work must have looked like a sketch of things to be done. It must have given him a glimpse of the philosophical possibilities of behaviorism. This glimpse has become increasingly important in Skinner's later work.

---

[13]See Skinner's <u>Autobiography</u> for details.

CHAPTER III

The Operant: A New Paradigm

Skinner builds on the work of Thorndike. The law of effect says that consequences have their effects upon behavior. Thorndike's application of this law resulted in one of the first efforts to obtain quantitative laws of behavior--the sort of quantitative laws which are characteristic of the physical sciences. Thorndike, with some famous experiments in which cats were placed in puzzle boxes, came up with laws of learning, or learning curves. The time it took for a cat to make the successful escape response was plotted against the number of trials or exposures the cat had to the problem situation--the puzzle box. This learning curve expressed a functional correlation between the dependent variable (time until successful response) and the independent variable (number of trials). Skinner gives Thorndike credit for this important step in the right (scientific) direction; but takes him to task for the misplaced emphasis attached to learning curves. Among the problems Skinner points to are (i) the important use made of the notion of success or successful and (ii) the interplay between the nature of Thorndike's apparatus and the opportunity for competing responses. The availability of competing responses would strongly affect the sort of learning curve obtained. In short, it is good to get quantitative laws, but the quantities involved in the laws must be chosen with greater care than Thorndike exhibited in his trial and error theory of learning.

Skinner's response to the mechanical deficiencies in Thorndike's experimental procedure was what has come to be known as the Skinner Box. The Skinner box is principally a compartment with two simple mechanisms, e.g., a bar to press, a disc to be pecked; and another apparatus to reward the animal for using the first apparatus, e.g., a food dispenser.

Predecessors and comparisions aside, let us
now look more closely at Skinner's approach. First
of all, what is it that the psychologist attempts
to explain or predict? For Skinner, it is particular responses. Explanation consists of subsum-
ing a particular response under some general law--
some principle of functional correlation. In even
vaguer terms, explanation consists of identifying
a particular response as belonging to a certain
class of responses. This class of responses would
be one we understand--one for which we have a law
or set of laws. Let us look at respondent, or
reflex behavior. We explain a particular response,
a knee jerk, by identifying it as belonging to the
class of knee-jerk responses. We understand this
class of knee jerk responses. We understand this
class of responses because we have the law of the
knee-jerk reflex. Put more schematically, a particular response r, is explained by identifying it
as a member of a class of responses r∅ where we
have a law s Ψ→ r ∅ (stimulus of kind Ψ elicits
response of kind ∅ ; or f(s Ψ)=r ∅ = the response
of kind ∅ is a function of an eliciting stimulus
of kind Ψ).

Now, all this could be put in the somewhat
neater, and certainly more 'establishment' terms of
the deductive or covering law model of explanation.
The particular response to be explained can be
viewed as the conclusion of a two premise argument:
the first premise comprises the covering law say
s Ψ→ r ∅ ; the particular response is covered
by the consequent term r ∅ (it is a member of the
class of r ∅). The second premise is the statement of conditions which in conjunction with the
covering law suffice to yield the response r_1 as
conclusion. In other words, the covering law
approach says two kinds, a stimulus kind and a
response kind, are linked in a certain way. It
identifies something as a stimulus of the above-
mentioned stimulus kind and permits the conclusion
that the response will be of the specified response
kind.

24

Having sketched the deductive or covering law model of explanation, we will work in what follows with the equivalent but pedagogically simpler notion of assimilation of members to class--reflex response-particular to response-type explained by the knee-jerk reflex--(a law of necessary connection between a tap on the knee stimulus and knee jerk response). In spite of all the verbiage, the problem of explaining reflex responses, or more precisely, unconditioned reflex responses, is a fairly simple matter. The strategy is: find the reflex! But things get more complicated when we realize that it is very difficult to distinguish between an unconditioned and conditioned response. In Pavlov's famous experiment, the unconditioned response (salivation-to-the-food) and the conditioned response (salivation-to-the-bell) are nearly indistinguishable. If the particular salivation response is a conditioned response, then our explanation will be somewhat more complicated. For the class to which the response is a member will be a class of conditioned responses. And the law which identifies or explicates this class will involve more than the unconditioned stimulus (food or tap on the knee) and the unconditioned response (salivation or knee jerk). What more will it involve? The short answer is that it will involve a conditioned or substitute stimulus. The longer answer would take us into an account of the conditioning process or the history of conditioning. The relation of conditioned stimulus to response is a matter of associating the desired conditioned stimulus to the unconditioned stimulus in such a way as to permit the conditioned stimulus to elicit the response in much the same way as did the unconditioned stimulus. The law here would in words go something like this: When a potential c.s.[14] is associated with an u.s. according to an appropriate schedule, it becomes a c.s. It can, then, substitute for the u.s. in eliciting the response in question.

---

[14] c.s. = conditioned stimulus.
u.s. = unconditioned stimulus.

Talk of schedule involves us in historical and biographical considerations, considerations in which
we were not involved in the case of explaining an
unconditioned response. An additional complication
is that just as many roads lead to Rome, there are
many classes of conditioned responses--many stimuli
which can be conditioned to elicit the same or very
similar responses. To attribute the conditioned
response to the right class must then involve the
history of conditioning, the biography of the
organism in question. We have been speaking in
terms of explanation but the parallel with prediction should be clear; indeed, the last point made
is even more dramatic when viewed in the context
of prediction. When it comes to conditioned or
learned responses, to predict what the organism
will do, we must look into its history.

We have been dealing with reflex-responses in
our attempt to understand the mechanisms of explanation in Skinnerian psychology. We formed a
general idea of explanation as the attribution of
a particular response to a class of responses.
The classes serve as things we understand, as
things by means of which we explain particulars.
Our understanding of these classes, in turn,
depends upon the availability of psychological laws
which serve to explain the class: The class of
unconditioned knee-jerk responses is explained or
better, explicated in terms of the psychological
law expressing the knee-jerk reflex. We saw further that these laws become more complicated,
involve historical or biographical considerations,
when it is conditioned rather than unconditioned
responses which we seek to explain.

We come now to the central and specific task
of Skinnerian psychology--the task of explaining
non-reflex responses; the task of explaining operant responses. It is only here that we come to
the fundamental problem of accounting for purposeful behavior. As might be expected, things become
increasingly complicated. Still, the general

26

idea of explanation developed above provides the framework for discussion.

In operant behavior, particular operant responses provide the subjects of explanation. They are explained to the extent that they can be identified as instances of operant response classes. For Skinner, an operant is primarily such a <u>class of responses</u>. The class of responses, the operant, is explicated by means of laws of operant behavior. In reflex or respondent behavior, the laws involve unconditioned eliciting stimuli, unconditioned responses, conditioned stimuli and conditioned responses--the last two implicitly involve a history of conditioning; a history of the association among stimuli. The laws of operant behavior involve other notions. The key idea is that of a <u>reinforcing stimulus</u>. The consequences of behavior--whether behavior gets rewarded, reinforced or not--play the crucial role in operant behavior. As an introductory statement, we can say that "the operant is defined by the property upon which reinforcement is made contingent."[15]

Take a pigeon in a Skinner Box. He is rewarded with a food pellet when and only when he pecks a disc. Now suppose we want to explain a particular pecking response. Take the first time he pecks the disc. Here we really have no explanation; the pigeon <u>just pecked</u> the disc. It is <u>prima facie</u> a spontaneous act. But he gets rewarded for this pecking and he pecks more frequently in consequence. Take now the 15th pecking response. In layman's terms we would say that he pecks (performs the fifteenth pecking) <u>in order to get</u> more food. More strictly, we could say he pecks because he has been rewarded for pecking in the past. The pigeon has, of course, been deprived of food--otherwise food would not serve as a reinforcer. Given this picture of things, how are we to explain the

---

[15]B. F. Skinner, <u>Science and Human Behavior</u>, p. 66.

pigeon's 15th pecking response? In one sense we
have explained this response by saying that he has
pecked because he has been rewarded by pecking.
This picks out the class of food-rewarded pecking
responses and identifies the 15th response as a
member of the class of responses. The law which
explicates the operant (the class of responses) is
the law relating pecking responses to reinforcement. There is some functional relation between
reinforcer (as independent variable) and pecking
response (as dependent variable). But this does
not give us a clear law. For what we have is
simply a report of the history of conditioning.
There has been a one-to-one relation between pecking and reward for 14 previous pecking responses.
But this is just the independent variable. What
depends upon this history of conditioning? What
does this history determine? In the case of respondent conditioning, the history caused (elicited)
the response. Here the connection is not a matter
of eliciting. It is a crucial problem for operant
psychology to choose an appropriate dependent variable. Once this is done we will have our laws.
Our laws will explicate operants, classes of responses, and we will thus be able to explain particular responses as instances of these classes.

In operant behavior we

> deal with variables which unlike the
> eliciting stimulus, do not 'cause' a
> given bit of behavior to occur but simply
> make the occurrence more probable. We
> may then proceed to deal for example,
> with the combined effect of more than one
> such variable.[16]

The laws of operant behavior which serve to explicate operants will differ from the laws of respondent behavior--reflexes--by virtue of the

---

[16]B. F. Skinner, Science and Human Behavior,
p. 62.

differences in independent and dependent variables. We already emphasized the central role of the reinforcing stimulus or reinforcer as independent variable in operant laws. Through a further process of conditioning the reinforcement itself can be made contingent on the presence of certain features in the environment. The pigeon, for instance, will receive food only when a red light is on. This red light comes to effectively control the pecking response. It provides an occasion upon which pecking is reinforced. It never quite elicits the response, however. The red light is termed a <u>discriminative stimulus</u>, an S^D. It is an additional independent variable. It in turn involves a history of conditioning. This history will inform us as to how the S^D and the reinforcer have been associated with one another. Historical considerations then involve not merely the schedule of reinforcement, but the circumstances in which the reinforcement take place. We can broaden the notion of <u>circumstance</u> to include in addition to the S^Ds, information about the state of the organism like its food situation.

So much for the independent variables. As dependent variable, Skinner takes <u>probability of response</u>. This is supposed to provide a measure of <u>tendency</u>, <u>propensity</u>, or <u>disposition</u> to respond. In respondent behavior we have an all or nothing situation; either the stimulus elicits the response or it does not. Here as we indicated it is a matter of making a response more probable. But this notion of probability of response produces some complications. The problem is: we observe sugar dissolving in water, but we do not observe the <u>solubility</u> of the sugar. The sugar is soluble even when it is not dissolving. Dispositional terms are difficult to fit into Skinner's framework, for the laws which explicate behavior are supposed to involve variables which are directly subject to observation and measurement. Notice that an operant itself is not directly observable. It is something abstract or theoretical. But it is supposed to be explicated in terms of laws which themselves

involve only observables as variables. Since an
adequate treatment of the problem of dispositional
terms would take us into the depths of contemporary
philosophy of science, we will discuss the problem
in as simple a way as possible.

We will go back briefly to Newton. Newton,
like Skinner, was an avowed observationalist, or
empiricist. He claimed to make no hypotheses. Yet
in his laws, we find variable quantities which are
not prima facie observables. Take what has come
down to us as Newton's second law of motion:
F = MxA (force = mass x acceleration). Acceleration is not a directly observable quantity. It is
the rate of change of velocity. We compute the
acceleration by means of the differential calculus.
The data for the computation are facts about velocity. Now these facts themselves happen to be
arrived at only through computation. After all,
velocity is simply another rate of change notion;
it is the rate of change of distance. We need the
differential calculus again. But we do finally get
to distance, which is not a rate. Information
about distances provides the data for computation
of velocity which in turn provides the data for the
computation of acceleration. If it is granted that
distance is a matter of direct measurement rather
than computation, (and this is not strictly speaking true), we see how a rather abstract quantity
can be grounded in something that is not abstract
at all. Acceleration is a theoretical notion.
Skinner's treatment of probability is roughly
analogous to the above sketched treatment of
acceleration. We do not observe probabilities, but
we do observe frequencies. Frequencies provide
the empirical data for probabilities. They legitimize the use of probabilities as dependent variables in laws of operant behavior.

Skinner admits that all is not simple when we
come to the observation and interpretation of
frequencies. In fact, this is for Skinner a
central problem for the experimental analysis of
behavior. To a large extent the Skinner Box was
designed to minimize difficulties with frequencies.

Frequency involves certain standard conditions.
The response in whose frequency we are interested
must not be interfered with appreciably. We want
our frequencies to be significant. We don't want
accidental features of the environment to rule them
out. If conditions, for instance, make it
extremely difficult for an organism to emit a certain response, then the frequency of emission will
hardly provide a reliable indication of tendency,
or propensity, or even probability under more nor-
mal or standard conditions. In the Skinner Box,
behavior will reach a fairly stable level. We will
then be able to investigate the frequency of some
selected response. There are important problems
with the notion of probability as Skinner employs
it. The preceding discussion was designed to permit us to ease our way through some of these. What
we need to hold on to is the following: Probability is a way of representing a frequency of
occurrence.

We should by now have a reasonable idea of the
way the Skinnerian account of operant behavior
works. It is an account which in Skinner's own
terms centers upon "the contingencies of reinforcement." What are these?

An adequate formulation of the interaction between organism and environment
must always specify three things: (1)
the occasion upon which a response
occurs, (2) the response itself, and
(3) the reinforcing consequences. The
interrelationships among them are the
 contingencies of reinforcement (my
emphasis).[17]

Some examples of these contingencies are schedules
of reinforcement (time intervals vs. response
ratios), superstition,--the rewarding of every nth

---

[17]B. F. Skinner, Contingencies of Reinforce-
ment--A Theoretical Analysis, p. 7.

response no matter what it may be, reinforcement itself, and avoidance. The Skinnerian psychologist provides analyses of these contingencies. Ultimately such analyses find their way into psychological laws, for the reader will no doubt have realized that contingencies of reinforcement all express certain interrelations between independent variables and the dependent variable-- probability of response. The contingencies of reinforcement approach represents a much more elaborate and flexible approach to behavior than stimulus-response theories (S-R theories). Such theories all have their roots in Watson, while Skinner's contribution mainly consists of setting Watson aside. Certainly Skinner speaks of stimulus and response; but stimuli are principally reinforcing and discriminative, responses are operant. And things other than stimuli enter into the Skinnerian account, e.g., historical or biographical variables--e.g., food deprivation. Skinner has really come a long way from the simple input/output conception of the reflex-arc, Watsonian behaviorism. Like Dewey's early theory of coordinations and Thorndike's trial and error learning theory, Skinner has emphasized the notion of feedback--the role consequences of behavior have upon behavior. When someone attaches the usually pejoratively intended label "S-R theorist" to Skinner, he usually does so out of ignorance. Caveat Lector.

There are some further features of Skinner's account which might appear strange and surprising, at least at first glance. One tends to think of the behaviorist as someone who attends strictly to the observable physical dimensions of behavior; as someone whose prime concern is with structure-- with the topography of behavior. Certainly this was true of Watson. This attitude was part and parcel of what Watson thought of as the scientific approach to psychology. It was probably E. C. Tolman who first got away from this emphasis upon topography by emphasizing the molar rather than the molecular dimension of behavior. For Tolman,

a molar account would have to involve so-called
intervening variables, things like purposes and
thoughts ('cognitive maps'). Skinner concentrates
neither on topography nor intervening variables.
For Skinner, a scientific account need not concentrate upon the topography of behavior and it should
not retreat to intervening variables; it should
rather concentrate upon the independent non-
intervening, the directly manipulable variables of
which behavior is a function.

There is a place for topographical considerations. Without their help we could not identify
particular responses. Topographical considerations are hardly sufficient, though , even for
this task. They do not by themselves tell us to
what operant, for example, a particular response
belongs. This is a matter of contingencies of
reinforcement--of the behavioral laws which explicate the operants. Or more straightforwardly, it
is a matter of the history of the organism which
emits the response. My scratching my nose as a
nervous habit and my scratching my nose to annoy
someone do not belong to the same operant, to the
same class of responses. They are, however, topographically indistinguishable. It is just this
kind of a case that causes serious trouble for a
topographically oriented approach. When Skinner
says that "the topography of an operant need not
be completely fixed, but some defining property
must be available to identify instances,"[18] what
he is saying is that it is convenient to employ a
topographical criterion as a necessary condition
for a response to count as belonging in a given
operant. A nose-scratching to annoy and a nose-
scratching as nervous habit must both involve the
scratching of the nose. But notice there is great
flexibility in identifying a topographical defining property or necessary condition. Skinner does,
however, appear to be committed to the position
that for something general like teasing to be an

_____

[18]B. F. Skinner, Contingencies of Reinforcement, p. 175.

operant, some topographical property common to all cases of teasing must be present. Such a property does not leap to mind. Perhaps such general modes of behavior are only operants in an extended sense. They can be viewed as abstract or theoretical operants (covering or summary operants) useful in organizing and systematizing the genuine, more specific operants--operants like teasing-by-nose-scratching. The reader will probably have realized that teasing is just the sort of thing whose ties to topography are minimal. It is much more a matter of the contingencies of reinforcement--the variables which control the indefinite behavior we call "teasing." It is also in this kind of case that one is likely to despair altogether of providing an adequate behaviorist account. Don't we have to bring in intentions, purposes and the like, if not as genuine mental phenomena, at least as intervening variables? (What makes teasing, we are tempted to say, is the intention to tease.) Skinner's answer is, of course, no. But we are not ready to examine the question at this point. It will have to be faced, however, and we shall do so in a forthcoming section devoted to purposes and intentions.

A further distinguishing feature of the Skinnerian approach is its emphasis upon the individual organism. It is usually the case that even the laws the Skinnerian discovers are laws relative to a specific organism. What Skinner tries to explain and predict (and control) are particular responses of individual organisms. There is no such thing as an average organism and a typical response. Most of Skinner's work is at a level analogous to physics' concern with eclipses of the sun, facts about specific bodies, and not to concern with eclipses in general. Why worry about a theory of eclipses in general, if we have laws governing the behavior of the particular bodies which interact to make the particular eclipse with which we are concerned? This attitude explains Skinner's frequently voiced antipathy towards statistical methods. They are simply unnecessary.

34

We can observe individual cases directly. And our problems are, after all, a matter exclusively of individual cases.

> The complex system we call an organism
> has an elaborate and largely unknown
> history which endows it with a certain
> individuality...Statistical techniques
> cannot eliminate this kind of indiv-
> iduality; they can only obscure and
> falsify it.[19]

Skinnerian behaviorism is distinguished from previous theories by the central role played by the term <u>operant</u>. It is at the same time the easiest and most difficult term to pin down in the Skinnerian lexicon. We can introduce the term by ostension--by examples--by positive and negative instances: writing a letter is an operant, a bicycle is not; kissing is, a match box is not; kicking a football to score a field goal is, a knee-jerk is not. At this level operants are actions or perhaps more accurately, actions which are not reflex in nature. They are the sort of things which come under Thorndike's law of effect rather than Pavlov's theory of reflexes. In fact, Skinnerian psychology can be viewed as a substan-tial elaboration upon Thorndike's law of effect. Skinnerian behaviorism is concerned with what the layman would term purposive or voluntary behavior--with what we can help doing rather than with what we can't help doing. But this way of introducing and characterizing the notion of <u>operant</u> is clearly rough and ready. How do we identify something as an operant? How do we distinguish one operant from another? These are questions which, properly speaking, belong to the science of psychology. An encyclopedia of operants would come at the end and

---

[19]B. F. Skinner, <u>Contingencies</u> <u>of</u> <u>Reinforce-</u><u>ment</u>, pgs. 111-112.

not at the beginning of psychological inquiry.
The layman usually can identify operants quite
well. But identification is not explanation.

The sort of analysis Skinner offers is causal
or functional in nature. The definition of an
operant does not, however, involve the appeal to
data of a physical (micro-physical), chemical,
neurophysiological or hypothestical sort. Though
behavior may be a function of such variables,
Skinner concentrates exclusively on certain kinds
of variables, principally publicly accessible
environmental variables.

The Skinnerian emphasis on operant behavior
was not in itself new. Dewey's notion of coordination as a corrective to the reflex-arc concept
certainly emphasized the purposive dimension of
behavior. Philosophers and psychologists who
talked about conduct (as Dewey himself came to do
in Human Nature and Conduct) were clearly working
with a conception of behavior close to Skinner's.
The most important psychologist to make much of
the operant conception without, however, using the
term operant was the previously mentioned E. C.
Tolman. Tolman emphasized a distinction between
conceptions, dimensions, or levels of behavior
which went back to C. D. Broad's The Mind and Its
Place in Nature. The distinction was that between
the molar and the molecular. For Tolman, as for
Skinner, behavior is a moral phenomenon.

> An act qua 'behavior' has distinctive
> properties all its own. These are to be
> identified and described irrespective of
> whatever muscular, glandular, or neural
> processes underlie them. These new
> properties, thus distinctive of molar
> behavior, are presumably strictly cor-
> related with, if you will, dependent
> upon, physiological motions. But

descriptively and per se they are other
than those motions.[20]

The emphasis is clearly anti-reductionist. The
laws of psychology deal with regularities on the
molar level. They need not be derived from putative neurophysiological or physical laws. This
amounts to the recognition of the autonomy of psy-
chology--or the autonomy of behavior as a field of
study. Tolman and Skinner both deal with behavior
as a molar phenomenon, i.e., they deal with purposive behavior. They differ in their accounts of
purposive behavior. For Tolman, purposive behavior involves purposes as entities. These entities
are admittedly objects which are not directly
encountered in observation or experiment; they are
rather hypothesized entities--postulated entities--
for the purpose of explaining purposive behavior.
These entities intervene between stimulus and response. They are intervening variables. On
Skinner's account, we do without purposes as entities; we provide an account of purposive behavior
without postulating purposes. This is part of
Skinner's attempt as a methodologist to dispense
with intervening variables altogether. Tolman
explicates purpose as an intervening variable
whereas Skinner eliminates purposes in his account
of purposive behavior.

One could certainly overemphasize the difference between Tolman and Skinner. The whole thing
centers upon how seriously intervening variables
are to be taken. It seems to be the case that for
Tolman the theory could in principle get along
without them; ultimately, intervening variables
are eliminable in terms of independent and dependent variables. (There are complications here
which philosophers of science have been struggling
with for some time.) Purposes and goals are what

---

[20]E. C. Tolman: "Behaviorism, A Molar
Phenomenon," Ch. I, Purposive Behavior in Animals
and Men, p. 8.

characterize molar behavior. Furthermore, to deal
with goals, cognitions, beliefs and perceptions
have to be taken into account--more intervening
variables. Still, when all is said and done evidence for psychological laws is always a matter of
independent and dependent variables. We attempt
to explain behavior by hypothesizing entities for
which our only evidence is behavior. But why take
the detour through intervening variables at all?
It seems that it is the theorist and not the theory
that requires the detour. The detour gives him a
picture of behavior which permits an understanding
that is not possible otherwise. This picture is
also supposed to serve as a fruitful source of
hypotheses. Taking the detour gives the theorist
ideas he would never get along the main road. The
Skinnerian would argue that the detour is likely to
do more harm than good. The psychologist ought to
be under the control of the data and not of the
hypothetical entities he postulates or abstracts
from the data. Purposes and cognitions are not
quite _things_ for Tolman. Their existence is more
shadowy than that. They are shadows cast by substantial independent and dependent variables. In
some sense the shadows are something...but then
again these somethings don't exist like other
things either.

> As an intervening variable, a cognition
> is not a thing. It is an abstraction
> defined by the theorist. While it is
> possible that physiologists may some day
> find some particular activity in the
> brain that corresponds to a cognition,
> this possibility is no concern of Tolman's.
> The meaning of the word 'cognitive' is
> determined by the definition that the
> theorist gives it. For Tolman, this defi-
> nition is in terms both of stimuli and

responses, since it intervenes between
them. Experience with certain stimuli
results in the formation of certain
cognitions.[21]

Note how even the last line seems to impute a real
or substantial status to the cognitions. It is
very difficult not to do this, but one should probably resist the temptation for abstractions do not
have locations in the way concrete objects do.
Tolman attempts to walk a narrow ridge between
behaviorism and traditional materialistic theories.
He seems to have room in his theory for both behavior and thought. The central place of thought or
cognition in his system is probably an illusion.
Talking about thought is simply a style, a manner
of talking about behavior. Some people insist upon
taking detours; Tolman insists upon a certain way
of talking about behavior.

We now have to present the fundamental ideas
of Skinnerian or operant psychology. Eventually
we will have to do some evaluation. We will need
criteria of adequacy or acceptability. This will
be no easy matter and it is this question that
lies at the heart of philosophical concern with
behaviorism. We will try to distinguish three
parts of the adequacy or acceptability problem.
First we have the question of adequacy as psychological science--or adequacy as a science of
man. Second we have the question of adequacy as a
philosophy of man. Here arises, for instance, the
question of whether an adequate theory of value or
approach to ethics can be provided within the
Skinnerian framework. And third we have the ultimate question: Does Skinnerian psychology replace

---

[21]W. F. Hill, Learning--A Survey of Psychological Interpretations, Chandler Publishing Co.,
1963, p. 117.

philosophy altogether? The three parts are not completely independent of one another but discussion will be facilitated by keeping them apart.

Does Skinner claim adequacy for his brand of behaviorism as a total philosophy? I think he does and inasmuch as he does he belongs to a tradition in philosophy which goes back principally to the 18th Century--the tradition can be labelled scientism. Scientism holds that all significant questions are scientific questions. Psychologism may be seen as a species of scientism. Philosophical questions (or more circumspectly, many philosophical questions) which have been traditionally viewed as basic philosophical questions are really psychological questions. This is especially the case insofar as the theory of knowledge, or epistemology, is concerned. This issue of psychologism will be the theme of our concluding chapter. The present task is to present and evaluate Skinnerian behaviorism as psychological science. But even here a precautionary word about the difficulty of the evaluative task is in order.

Two dimensions of scientific critique may be distinguished. First the methodological side. Skinnerian psychology has its own ideas about proper scientific method. Its historic roots are in Bacon and Newton; its contemporary roots (with some reservations) are in operationism and positivism, especially 20th Century logical positivism. This attitude towards method no doubt affects the standards of clarity and intelligibility for acceptable scientific work. But there is also the more indirect effect upon choice of subject matter or problem selection. Methodological considerations affect aims and procedures as well as conceptions of scientific explanation. They also significantly affect what is taken to be the subject matter of investigation. Put in the form of a slogan: they affect the forms explanations take as well as what gets explained. So it is difficult to separate Skinnerianism as a philosophy of science from Skinnerianism as a science of psychology.

40

Though methodological considerations affect what is taken to be the scientific task, this does not mean that differing methodological approaches cannot or will not converge upon a common task, a common set of problems. There does seem to be at least a common denominator which could serve as the task of psychology, for instance. This would be the explanation (including description) of human behavior--conduct, action or some other roughly equivalent phenomenon. Some psychologists think they have to speak of explaining thought and behavior. But we are interested in finding a common-denominator, a yard-stick for comparison. Everyone could at least agree upon thoughtful-behavior as what requires an account--an explanation. This is a less presumptuous conception than thought and behavior. If every different psychological approach were working with a different set of problems, then these approaches would be in an important way incommensurable. Skinner and Tolman are both concerned with purposeful behavior. But it would be definitely misleading in Skinner's case (and possibly misleading in Tolman's case) to say that he is concerned with behavior and purpose(s). Different approaches to purposeful behavior needn't be commensurable concept by concept. (A Tolmanian purpose needn't have some specific Skinnerian correlate.) Furthermore, scientific explanations of behavior needn't present us with substitutes for each and every concept employed in our everyday theorizing or our talk about human behavior. To ask for a scientific explication of the concepts we ordinarily employ in talking about human action (and thought) would be to ask it to show itself superfluous. The task of scientific psychology is after all not simply to explicate our ordinary conceptual framework; it is rather to improve upon it. Its task is revisionary. Furthermore, if there is one thing contemporary philosophical psychology has amply shown, it is that even the explicative task is no easy matter.

CHAPTER IV

Skinner and the Inside Story

We have been dealing with what goes into a
Skinnerian account of behavior. It is time to
turn explicitly to what gets left out, and to some
further peculiarities of the account. With all
Skinner's talk of contingencies of reinforcement,
isn't something of great importance ignorned altogether? Doesn't an adequate account have to deal
with what goes on inside the organism? Doesn't it
have to tell the inside story too? Skinner admits
that the temptation to get inside is considerable.
For one thing, Skinnerian variables are historical
in nature. These variables are the 'causes' of
behavior, but no bridge is built between what happened in the organism's past and what the organism
does in the present. We want to see just how the
past is linked with present behavior. We want to
see real, substantial causes. We want to see the
necessary connections (something, of course, David
Hume tried to show we could never see anyway). A
further reason for the attraction the inside story
has for us is that it is inside--below the surface; in Skinner's terms it is a "deep dark
secret." For Skinner, the temptation to get
inside is to be resisted. We will come to his
reasoning shortly.

Actually, there does not seem to be an inside
story so much as many inside stories. Our friend,
the mentalist or dualist, has his own special
inside story. For the mentalist what we need is
to get inside the mind. And we need special
capabilities to do this--introspection or philosophical speculation. From Plato through Augustine
and Descartes and up through some forms of present
day cognitive psychology the mentalist inside
story has dominated. It has its problems, as
almost anyone, including the mentalist, will admit.
Yet the claim is, I think, that this kind of
inside story is unavoidable. Phenomena, like

43

thought, purpose and intention can only be explained by a mentalist account, so the claim goes. Even William James couldn't resist features of this mentalist line. As we saw, E. C. Tolman has, to some extent, been touched by it, though it would be stretching things to pin the label "mentalist" on him. Skinner has always been wary of this dimension of Tolman's approach. What Tolman couldn't resist was locating his intervening variables somewhere--the somewhere was the mind.

> At first glance, Edward Tolman seems to have moved well beyond a stimulus-response formula. He made no use of eliciting stimuli, describing his rats as 'docile'. He turned from topography of response to goal-directedness, and used apparatus which emphasized purpose...But he put the 'third' variables inside the organism, where they 'intervened' between stimulus and response. There was no reason to do this except to maintain something like the old reflex pattern. His intervening variables quickly assumed the function of mental processes (as they were essentially designed to do), and it is not surprising that they have been warmly taken up by cognitive psychologists.[22]

We will come back to mentalism when we deal explicitly with the Skinnerian analysis of purpose as a paradigm for elimination of mental phenomena.

There is another inside story with nearly as long and distinguished a history as the mentalistic one. This is the materialist or neurophysiological inside story. Many would claim that it is this inside story which will carry the future. Admittedly, there is something 'scientific',

---

[22]B. F. Skinner, <u>Contingencies of Reinforcement</u>, p. 28.

hard-nosed, and tough-minded about the appeal to
the brain. The Skinnerian account leaves the
brain and its helpers out. No appeal is made to
what Skinner terms "physiological man." All this
might come as something of a surprise to those who
see Skinner as the outstanding representative of
the materialist or mechanist approach to man.
Here, where so many have jumped at the chance of
turning mind into matter, Skinner resists. It is
not that mind resists being turned into matter,
but that both the mind theory and its materialist
substitute are unnecessary and for the most part
harmful to the study of behavior.

As was indicated, the materialist story has
itself a long history. It is rooted in pre-
Socratic speculation and gets some impetus from
Aristotle's psychological and biological speculations, as well as from the work of medieval
physician-philosophers like Avicenna and Peter of
Spain. It only really gains impetus after things
begin to change in physics. Physical things become
more mechanical. The 17th Century English philosopher, Thomas Hobbes, was perhaps the first to try
to reduce all mental phenomena to matter and
motion. The Hobbesian dream dominated the work of
La Mettrie and De Holbach in the age of Enlightenment and still apparently has great attraction for
contemporary hard-nosed philosophers. This last
point can be underlined by all the contemporary
interest in the so-called "identity theory" of the
relation of mind and body. Witness the following
from a significant contemporary essay on the mind-
body problem:

If the materialist can adapt the adverbial
metaphysical position associated with the
sensory terminology, then he need not
worry about Hobbes' phantasms or sensations, and the problem about the properties sensations have but brain phenomena
lack. This would be an important gain,
because this problem seems intractable.
He is indeed left with the problem of the

45

properties which sensings and Hobbes'
'internal-motions', or brain events,
might not have in common, but this problem may be solvable.[23]

Skinner has long been sceptical about the
neurological inside story. In his early 1938 The
Behavior of Organisms, he devotes a chapter to the
central nervous system--C.N.S.--and suggests that,
given the available hard data neurophysiologists
possess about this system, it would be perhaps better to say "C.N.S." stood for the conceptual
nervous system--a neurophysiological construct, or
scientific fiction. The good thing about neurophysiology is that it is unquestionably physical.
The bad thing is that it is such a poorly understood system. Even the man in the street jumps
easily to neurophysiology for an explanation of
behavior. This, too, has a long history.

Cervantes contended that Don Quixote's
troubles were neurological. His brain
was 'distempered', 'out of order', 'turned
topsy turvy' and 'dried out' (by sleep-
ing little and reading much, the moisture
of his brain was exhausted to that degree
that at last he lost the use of his reason). His uncle's brains were cracked...
Cervantes may have been poking fun at
physiology, but if so, we have not learned
the lesson.[24]

The key question that Skinner asks about
neurophysiology and its relation to behavior seems
to be the following: How would laws of operant
psychology be modified through the introduction of

---

[23]James Cornman, "On the Elimination of Sensations," Review of Metaphysics, September 1968,
p. 35.

[24]B. F. Skinner, Contingencies of Reinforcement, p. 281.

additional neurophysiological independent variables? Let us schematically represent an operant law: $f(i_1...i_n) = h(r)$ where $i_1...i_n$ are independent variables and $h(r)$ is the dependent variable, probability of response. Suppose we add a new, neurophysiological independent variable j. How will this affect our previous law? There are a number of possibilities. If we have direct evidence of the way j contributes to behavior; if we can manipulate this variable in such a way as to allow us to perform experiments (and this is no easy matter for people are reluctant to walk about with electrodes in their head), then we will simply have a new behavioral law of the form $f(i_1,...i_n j) = h(r)$. Note that it is not the case that the old law has been refuted. We simply have a new law which makes use of additional information. The old law said that probability of response is a function f of the specified independent variables $i,...i_n$. The new law says that probability of response is a function--a new function--of the specified variables including the additional neurophysiological variable j. In fact, it is not unreasonable to say that our old law might do just fine for purposes of predicting and controlling human behavior.

Skinner admits, I think, that ultimately a total science of human behavior will include all the independently specifiable information of a neurophysiological or, more generally, of an inside variety. The important thing to see is that the Skinnerian psychologist does not depend upon some future neurophysiological science for its own laws. At best, neurophysiology can give us new laws. It cannot refute the behavioral laws. In fact, it is behavioral law (the old kind of law) which gives the neurophysiologist the clue as to what to investigate, as to what needs explanation. "A behavioral analysis is essentially a statement of the facts to be explained by studying the nervous system." On the other hand, "we can predict and control behavior without knowing how dependent and independent variables are connected."[25] In a more advanced account of a behaving organism the historical variables will give way to causal or contemporary connecting variables. If and when we can observe something like the momentary states of an organism, we will be able to use it and not its history to predict behavior. Still the history of the organism and the behavioral laws involving them form the only ladder by which we will get the momentary state of an organism. We must first have laws correlating momentary-state behavioral laws.

But we are not finished with out question as to how the laws of operant psychology would be modified throughout the introduction of additional independent neurophysiological variables. In one sense of _intervening_ neurophysiological variables are clearly intervening. They intervene between stimulus, history of conditioning, and response. In the preceding paragraph we treated these variables as real, i.e., independently accessible to observation and/or measurement. The reader will recall that Tolman's intervening variables were not real in this sense. They were conceptual in the sense of Skinner's tongue-in-cheek _conceptual nervous system_. In the case of what we might term conceptual intervening variables, we seem to have two subcases: (1) the intervening variables are inferred from and completely eliminable in terms of our independent behavioral (historical) variables (ii) they are inferred from but go beyond, (are not eliminable in terms of), our independent variables. If subcase (i) then the addition of the new neurophysiological variable changes the old law not at all. Because of eliminability we recall, we really have just the old law. If (ii) then the introduction of such a variable represents an unjustified leap beyond the data. It adds something to the law all right--but what it adds is, for Skinner illegitimate, as are the new laws.

[25]B. F. Skinner, _Contingencies of Reinforcement_, p. 283.

Explanations in terms of inner states or agents, however, may require some further comment. To what extent is it helpful to be told 'He drinks because he's thirsty'? If to be thirsty means nothing more than to have a tendency to drink, this is mere redundancy. If it means that he drinks because of a state of thirst, an inner causal event in invoked. If this state is purely inferential--if no dimensions are assigned to it which would make direct observation possible--it cannot serve as an explanation. But if it has physio-logical or psychic properties, what role can it play in a science of behavior?[26]

Skinner's objections to the inside story, then, do not amount to denying that there is such a story. When we speak about functional laws, laws of oper-ant behavior, we can do so only because there are organisms with insides to which our laws apply. Different insides, different organisms or differ-ent species permit different laws. The Skinnerian account doesn't deal explicitly with the inside story--with variables pertaining to the insides of the organism. But the laws obtained would not be what they are unless these laws characterized organisms with insides. The very value of the function relating independent and dependent vari-ables depends upon the inside story, or presupposes an inside story in the sense that experiment would probably yield different functional relations between outside story variables if organisms with different insides were the subject of experiment. It is not assumed that the organism is a black box, if this requires the organism to be empty--to have no insides. For if our organisms had no insides, there would be no behavioral laws forthcoming at all. There would be no organisms and hence

———————

[26]B. F. Skinner, Science and Human Behavior, p. 33.

nothing to experiment with. Skinner summarizes
the matter of inner states as follows:

> The objection to inner states is not
> that they do not exist, but that they
> are not relevant in a functional analy-
> sis. We cannot account for the behavior
> of any system while staying wholly inside
> it; eventually we must turn to forces
> operating on the organism from without.
> Unless there is a weak spot in our causal
> chain so that the second link is not law-
> fully determined by the first, or the
> third by the second, then the first and
> third links must be lawfully related. If
> we must always go back beyond the second
> link for prediction and control, we may
> avoid many tiresome and exhausting
> digressions by examining the third link
> as a function of the first. Valid infor-
> mation about the second link may throw
> light upon this relationship but can in
> no way alter it.[27]

NATURE/NURTURE: Sometimes the attempt is made to
identify behaviorism with certain features of old-
fashioned Lockean empiricism. The behaviorist is
charged with having inherited the Lockean rejection of innate ideas; indeed, with having rejected
inner states or entities altogether. The claim is
that for the behaviorist all is a matter of nurture or learning and nothing a matter of nature or
heredity. Now while this charge might have some
validity in connection with Watson's behaviorism,
it fails completely to appreciate the Skinnerian
position. This position is closely tied to
Skinner's views on the inside story which we discussed above. Skinner does not deny the existence
of an inside story. In fact, he presupposes such
a story. But he doesn't take this story explicitly into account by providing place for inside

---

[27]B. F. Skinner, <u>Science and Human Behavior</u>,
p. 35.

story variables in behavioral laws. Nothing in the Skinnerian approach requires the rejection of nature in favor of nurture.

> The basic issue is not whether behavior is instinctive or learned, as if these adjectives described essences, but whether we have correctly identified the variables responsible for the pro- venance of behavior as well as those currently in control.

> Early behaviorists, impressed with the importance of newly discovered environ- mental variables, found it particularly reinforcing to explain what appeared to be an instinct by showing that it could have been learned, just as ethologists have found it reinforcing to show that behavior attributed to the environment is still exhibited when environmental variables have been ruled out. The important issue is empirical: what _are_ the relevant variables?[28]

Williard Van Orman Quine, a distinguished contem- porary philosopher (and friend and colleague of Skinner) who shares with Skinner a commitment to the externalized empiricism of contemporary behaviorism, puts the matter in an especially charming and illuminating way:

> For, whatever we may make of Locke, the behaviorist is knowingly and cheer- fully up to his neck in innate mechanisms of learning readiness. The very reinforce- ment and extinction of responses, so central to behaviorism, depends on prior inequalities in the subjects' qualitative spacing so to speak, of stimulations. If

---

[28]B. F. Skinner, Contingencies of Reinforce- ment, p. 199.

the subject is rewarded for responding
in a certain way to one stimulation and
punished for thus responding to another
stimulation, then his responding in the
same way to a third stimulation reflects
an inequality in his qualitative spacing
of the three stimulations; the third must
resemble the first more than the second.
Since each learned response presupposes
some such prior inequalities, some such
inequalities must be unlearned; hence
innate. Innate biases and dispositions
are the corner stone of behaviorism, and
have been studied by behaviorists.[29]

We may come back now to Russell's challenge.
Russell's Philosophy attempted to push the behaviorist or objective approach as far as possible.
In this attempt serious limitations were discov-
ered. A number of these centered upon the area of
perception. In broad lines, Russell concluded
that the objective approach needed to be supplemented with a subjective-introspective approach.
Introspection has always gone hand in hand with
the traditional mentalistic approach to psychology.
It is in this sphere of mental acts--of thinking
and perceiving--where Russell found behaviorism
wanting. As we suggested earlier, Skinner's neo-
behaviorism can in part be treated as an attempt
to respond to Russell's challenge. It is to
Skinner's response that we now turn, with special
emphasis on the problem of perception. The discussion will focus on seeing as the key species of
perception.

---

[29]W. V. O. Quine, "Linguistics and Philosophy"
in Language and Philosophy, edited by Sidney Hook
(New York, 1969).

In "Behaviorism at Fifty,"[30] Skinner tries to
show how far Behaviorism has come since Watson's
1913 manifesto. The effort is largely a matter of
responding to Russell's challenge--though Skinner
does not put the matter in this way. The essence
of his view on perception is: Perception is behavior. This requires unpacking. We will speak in
terms of seeing. Suppose a boy sees a dog; it is
not obvious that there is any behavior which can
be fittingly labelled seeing-a-dog. Still there
are any number of things the boy might do which
depend upon seeing a dog. He might say "Look a
dog" to his father next to him. He might simply
say it to himself. He might walk across the street
to avoid the dog. He might continue straight ahead
so that he can pat the dog. He might take out pen-
cil and paper from his briefcase and begin making
a sketch of the dog. We will not multiply examples
beyond necessity. Now, none of these responses
constitute seeing-a-dog, but on the Skinnerian
account there is no seeing-a-dog in abstraction
from responses such as these. There is something
which all these responses share but which is not
itself a response or piece of behavior--and this
is a matter of stimulus control. All these responses are under the control of the dog present.
The dog is the discriminative stimulus--the S^D.
The behavior of seeing a dog may then be understood
as the class of responses under the control of the
S^D dog. When we talk of the boy being under the
control of the S^D dog, we are saying that the boy
discriminates the dog. But discrimination by
itself is simply a matter of the stimulus controlling behavior and not anything the boy himself
does. There is then no specific response seeing-
a-dog that is not some member of the class of responses which are under the control of the S^D dog.
The above analysis, which is perhaps more explicit
than what Skinner offers, treats seeing (perceiving) as an operant, or more accurately, a higher

---

[30]B. F. Skinner, Contingencies of Reinforcement, Ch. 9.

order operant or class of operants. As such, the account might be one-sided in the following way. There could be some respondent (reflex) features of seeing, i.e.: Some response or responses might be simply triggered or elicited by the dog when the light waves it transmits impinge upon the eye. We might term these responses <u>sensing responses</u> and distinguish sensing from perceiving. These sensings might well be private events. But as we shall see <u>privacy</u> does not itself make an event a <u>non-grata</u> for Skinner. (Here is one place where Skinner's neo-behaviorism and classical behaviorism part ways.)

We have at least a working sketch of the Skinnerian account of seeing as behavior. It is particularly interesting for what it <u>does not</u> contain. The account does not involve any copies or representation of external objects which the perceiver observes or develops like a photographic negative.

> At some point the organism must do more
> than create duplicates. It must see,
> hear, smell, and so on, as forms of <u>action</u>
> rather than of <u>reproduction</u>. <u>It must do</u>
> <u>some of the things it is differentially</u>
> <u>reinforced for doing when it learns to</u>
> <u>respond discriminatively.</u>[31]

The world we perceive is the world around us in the sense that the S^D's which control perception of behavior belong to the world around us. However, (and this is important), we may be under the control of an S^D when the S^D is no longer present. The perception-behavior is, however, usually learned when the S^D is in fact present. On Skinner's account, we can see dogs where there are no dogs present. This occurs when the behavior of seeing-a-dog which was learned in the presence of

---

[31]B. F. Skinner, <u>Contingencies</u> <u>of</u> <u>Reinforce-</u><u>ment</u>, p. 232.

dogs is occasioned by some feature in the environment which makes the behavior of seeing dogs more probable. In other words, other S^D's besides actual dogs might come to control the behavior of seeing-a-dog. We will return to this momentarily. To summarize, seeing as behavior involves (1) contingencies relalating external stimuli and overt responses and (ii) private accompaniments of either operant or respondent character.

With the above as background the following important passage from Behaviorism at Fifty should be comprehensible.

> It is usually easiest to see a friend
> when we are looking at him, because
> visual stimuli similar to those present
> when behavior was acquired exert maximal
> control over the response. But mere
> visual stimulation is not enough; even
> after being exposed to the necessary
> reinforcement, we may not see a friend
> who is present unless we have reason to
> do so. On the other hand, if the reasons
> are strong enough, we may see him in some-
> one bearing only a superficial resemblance
> or when no one like him is present at all.
> If conditions favor seeing something else,
> we may behave accordingly. If, on a hunt-
> ing trip, it is important to see a deer,
> we may glance towards our friend at a
> distance, see him as a deer, and shoot.[32]

We have come this far without talking about the supposed "stubborn fact of consciousness." We have been able to do this because it is not seeing, according to Skinner, which raises the question of consciousness, but seeing that we are seeing. There are any number of natural contingencies which teach man to see. Only people, the

---

[32]B. F. Skinner, The Contingencies of Reinforcement, p. 233.

verbal community, can teach man to see that he
sees. It is the verbal community which produces
'consciousness'. Basically, consciousness consists in responding to our own responses: to
learn that we see is to learn to respond to our
seeing in the ways the verbal community teaches us,
and to answer questions (What did you see?), for
instance. We are not unconscious of the fact that
much more can be said about consciousness.

Since seeing does not require things seen, we
can treat dreaming and some cases of simple recall
as seeing. It is the preoccupation with <u>objects</u>
of perception which has dominated the western
psychological tradition. This tradition has given
us such gems as Plato's aviary and our everyday
storehouse of memory. In other words, this emphasis has provided us with the root metaphor for any
number of inadequate psychologies. What would
happen to Plato's reminiscence theory, Augustine's
illumination theory, and the Cartesian theory of
the natural light if perception and understanding
were treated as behavior?

It took man a long time to understand
that when he dreamed a wolf, no wolf
was actually there. It has taken him
much longer to understand that not even
a representation of a wolf is there.[33]

This gives us some idea of how Skinner responds to
Russell's challenge. Skinnerian behaviorism is a
much more developed theory than Russell's, Watson's
and Thorndike's. Also, Skinner does not reject
introspection out-right as did classical behaviorism. Skinner actually attempts to incorporate
some feature of Russell's subjective method into
his own account. What he tries to avoid, however,
is any tinge of traditional mentalism in his dealing with private events.

---

[33]B. F. Skinner, <u>Contingencies of Reinforce-</u>
<u>ment</u>, p. 234.

It is important to emphasize that for Skinner
we are not to refuse data simply on the grounds
that a second observer cannot see or feel them
without the help of instruments.

> One _solution_, (to the problem of pri-
> vate events--italics mine) often regarded
> as behavioristic, is to grant the distinc-
> tion between public and private events
> and rule the latter out of scientific
> consideration. This is a congenial solu-
> tion for those to whom scientific truth
> is a matter of convention or agreement
> among observers. It is essentially the
> line taken by logical positivism and
> physical operationism.[34]

This would be an appropriate time to tie up
some loose ends. The Skinnerian account attempts
to deal with purposeful, goal-directed behavior
without invoking purposes or goals as special
entities of either mentalist or neurophysiological
kind. Purposeful behavior is not something which
consists of purposes grafted onto topographical
structures. Purpose is not a property of the
structure of behavior, it is rather a way of refer-
ring to the controlling variables. As the reader
will recall, purpose is treated by Skinner--
following Thorndike--as involving the effects of
consequences upon behavior. But this is not a
case of the future affecting the present or past,
a principle which once dominated an immature physics. It is the operant as a class of behavior,
rather than the response as a particular instance,
which is conditioned. The usual move to get
around the notion of final cause--the causal
efficacy of the future--involves transforming a
future cause into a present idea or neurophysiological configuration and locating these in the
mind or brain. The future cause is replaced by a
present idea of a future cause. Tolman, as we saw,

---

[34]B. F. Skinner, Contingencies of Reinforcement, p. 226.

seems to lean in this direction. But Skinner will have none of this. We are not to say that a man behaves either because of the consequences which are to follow his behavior or because of his present idea of the consequences which are to follow his behavior. "We simply say that he behaves because of the consequences which <u>have</u> followed similar behavior in the past. This is, of course, the Law of Effect or operant conditioning."[35] Just as some would argue that purposeful behavior in general cannot be explained without purposes, others would say that looking for something, for example, must invoke the something looked for as relevant to the explanation of the behavior. Of course, the something-looked-for need not even exist (the honest man of Diogenes), and philosophers have joyfully spilled some ink over <u>intentionally inexistent objects</u>. This kind of philosophizing is hardly attractive for Skinner.

> Suppose we condition a pigeon to peck a
> spot on the wall of a box and then, when
> the operant is well established, remove
> the spot. The bird now goes to the
> usual place along the wall. It raises
> its head, cocks its eye in the usual
> direction, and may even emit a weak peck
> in the usual place. Before extinction
> is very far advanced it returns to the
> same place again and again in similar
> behavior. Must we say that the pigeon
> is 'looking for the spot'? Must we take
> the looked-for spot into account in explain-
> ing the behavior?[36]

---

[35]B. F. Skinner, <u>Science and Human Behavior</u>, p. 87.

[36]<u>Ibid</u>., p. 89.

Skinner's conclusion is that, "in general,
looking for something consists of emitting responses which in the past have produced 'something'
as a consequence."[37] Since sometimes when we look
for something we seem to see the thing not neces-
sarily in some place, but in the sense of having
some picture of what we are looking for, Skinner's
account here would have to be supplemented with
something like his account of seeing. Looking for
something would then involve some kind of seeing
behavior, and instead of saying we are under the
control of an intentionally inexistent wallet, for
example, when we are looking for our wallet, we
could say we are (partially) under the control of
the behavior, or some species of behavior, seeing-
a-wallet. Even on this extended account we keep
within the operant framework of variables responsible for behavior. No current goals, purposes,
or non-existent objects are brought into the
account.

---

[37]Ibid.

PART II

CHAPTER V

Freedom and Dignity

Philosophers have spilled much ink on the question of freedom. It is safe to say that freedom means different things to different people-- there are many conceptions of freedom. Skinner says we are beyond freedom. What we have to be clear on is just what we are beyond. There is a 'freedom from' which for Skinner amounts to freedom from aversive control which is a freedom we are certainly not beyond. There are certain stimuli which an organism turns away from (stimuli the removal of which increases the probability of a response contingent upon such removal); such stimuli are called negative reinforcers. When we are under the control of such reinforcers we are in aversive situations, situations which we try to avoid altogether, or failing this, try to escape from when we are in them.

> The struggle to avoid aversive situa-
> tions is a legitimate struggle for
> freedom. We are certainly not beyond
> this. This kind of 'struggle for free-
> dom' is mainly directed toward intentional
> controllers--towards those who treat
> others aversively in order to induce them
> to behave in particular ways. Thus a child
> may stand up to his parents, a citizen may
> overthrow a government, a communicant may
> reform a religion, a student may attach a
> teacher or vandalize a school, and a drop-
> out may work to destroy a culture. (BFAD,
> 27)[38]

---

[38]All references in text are to B. F. Skinner's Beyond Freedom and Dignity, (Bantam Book Company), 1972.

A "literature of freedom," Skinner informs us, has grown up with the intention of getting people to avoid or escape from people who control them aversively. This goal is legitimate. It has had much success. But there is an idea (ideological) content to this literature which causes trouble. There has been considerable emphasis put upon feelings and states of mind. Freedom is treated as a possession.

> A person escapes from or destroys the power of a controller in order to feel free, and once he feels free and can do what he desires, no further action is recommended and none is prescribed by the literature of freedom, except perhaps eternal vigilance lest control be resumed. (30)

The feeling of freedom comes to replace the technique for escaping from aversive situations as the primary concern. This weakens the effectiveness of the literature of freedom in the following way. When aversive measures become more subtle, when the controllers get more clever, the feeling of freedom is frequently untouched. Aversive consequences may be postponed, for instance. We get less free, but we still feel just as free.

> The literature of freedom has never come to grips with techniques of control which do not generate escape or counterattack because it has dealt with the problem in terms of states of mind and feelings...Freedom is a matter of contingencies of reinforcement, not of the feelings the contingencies generate. The distinction is particularly important when the contingencies do not generate escape or counterattack. (35)

The legitimate struggle for freedom, according to Skinner, is the struggle to escape and avoid aversive control. The literature of freedom is ineffective in dealing with subtle forms

of aversive control, control involving deferred
aversive consequences. It is one thing to struggle to avoid aversive control, it is quite
another thing to struggle to avoid control altogether. This later struggle is doomed to failure.
Control is always there, positive or aversive,
direct or subtle. To say this, is to say nothing
more than human behavior is law-like. Cause and
not caprice reigns. The literature of freedom has
had, Skinner tells us, a crucial deleterious side-
effect. It has led to a certain overkill. It has
fostered the attempts to escape from all control
whatever. It has tried to make any indication of
control aversive.

> Those who manipulate human behavior are
> said to be evil men, necessarily bent
> on exploitation. Control is clearly
> the opposite of freedom, and if freedom
> is good, control must be bad. What is
> overlooked is control which does not
> have aversive consequences at any time. (38)

We are then beyond freedom, when _freedom_ is taken
to mean _beyond control_. It is self-defeating for
man to mistake the struggle for freedom from
aversive control for the struggle for freedom from
control altogether. If we do this, we will never
be able to solve the major problems facing human
culture. Solutions demand some kind of effective
control. They demand a technology of human
behavior.

We are beyond freedom in the sense of freedom
from control; so we might as well face the
realities of control. We are also, even more
shockingly perhaps, beyond dignity.

> Any evidence that a person's behavior
> may be attributed to external circum-
> stances seems to threaten his dignity
> or worth. We are not inclined to give
> a person credit for achievements which
> are in fact due to forces over which he
> has no control...But as an analysis of

behavior adds further evidence, the
achievements for which a person himself is to be given credit seem to
approach zero, and both the evidence
and the science which produces it are
then challenged. (41)

Freedom involves responsibility, dignity involves
credit. It is not enough to take away man's responsibility for evil, we must also take away his
credit for good. People usually receive credit
for their actions when the action appears to come
from, to be caused by, the person himself, where
external causes of the action are inconspicuous.
People do not get credit for sneezing or cough-
ing, for instance. (We assume, of course, this
behavior is respondent and not "put on" or "pretend.") The more uncanny or inexplicable an act
which does good, the more credit accrues to the
initiator. Of course, giving credit serves as a
reinforcer for the piece of behavior upon which
the credit is made contingent. We want children
to be able to do arithmetic, let us say, without
using their fingers (or toes) and so we reward
them with more credit for this desirable form of
behavior than for digital arithmetic. It is also
the case, of course, that in mental arithmetic as
opposed to digital arithmetic, the controlling
discriminative stimuli are not obvious. In
reflexes, the controlling stimuli are obvious and
praise or credit can only be brought to bear on
the response with great difficulty. These are two
good reasons for withholding credit. We employ
credit only when it can effectively serve to
modify behavior. "Good husbandry may also explain
why we do not commend people who are obviously
working simply for commendation. Behavior is to
be commended only if it is more than merely com-
mendable."(48) Fairness and justice in one sense
at least involve the notion of desert or merit.
Desert seems to involve the idea of good
husbandry--keeping rewards commensurate with the
requirements for maintaining behavior. We do not
want to be inefficient--to be either profligate or
miserly with our rewards. Perhaps more

importantly desert involves the conspicuousness of controlling variables. We don't want to reward the person when the stars, his genes, or his upbringing deserve the credit. Skinner emphasizes that there is something more than good husbandry involved in our concern with dignity and fairness. We do not merely praise and give credit for actions, we frequently marvel at them. We marvel at actions and admire the agents. "We stand in awe of the inexplicable, and it is therefore not surprising that we are likely to admire behavior more as we understand it less. And, of course, what we do not understand we attribute to autonomous man." (49) When we don't understand behavior--mathematical creativity--for instance, we are at a loss to know how exactly to reproduce it or strengthen it. All we can reasonably do is resort to admiration. This at least should help in encouraging the behavior.

Just as there is a struggle for freedom (in both the legitimate sense of struggle against aversive control and the illegitimate (extended) sense of struggle against control altogether-- there is also a struggle for dignity. A literature of dignity goes along with it. This literature aims at identifying practices and people which receive credit from us. When we make things easy for people--when we use programmed texts or teaching machines in education--we limit the chances for credit. Why any idiot could learn the material if it is presented this way! When we make things really tough, on the other hand, there is plenty of opportunity for credit. The literature of dignity likes heroes and heroism, as such

  it conflicts here with the literature
  of freedom, which favors a reduction
  in aversive features of daily life, as
  by making behavior less arduous, dangerous, or painful, but a concern for personal worth sometimes triumphs over
  freedom from aversive stimulation--for

65

example, when quite apart from medical
issues, painless childbirth is not as
readily accepted as painless dentistry.
(53)

The literature of dignity, then, on Skinner's
view, stands in the way of human progress. It too
will have to go. It fears a technology of behavior, because it will decrease chances for credit
and admiration. It prefers mystery cum dignity.

We have already encountered two notions of
freedom--the legitimate, according to Skinner,
freedom from aversive control, and the illegitimate, freedom from control simpliciter. Skinner
begins his discussion of punishment by identifying
still another notion of freedom--freedom from
physical restraint. Now, physical restraint is
certainly aversive--removal of such restraints can
be employed to increase the probability of an
action for the performance of which the removal is
made contingent. But not all aversive control
involves physical restraint. "Physical restraint
is an obvious condition, which seems particularly
useful in defining freedom, but with respect to
important issues, it is a metaphor and not a very
good one." (56) Philosophers from the time of
Thomas Hobbes to the present have attempted to
reconcile freedom with determinism by defining
freedom as freedom to do what one wills. One is
free to do what one wills to the extent that one
isn't physically restrained from doing what one
wills. One is so restrained when one is physically compelled to do something else incompatible
with what one wills. The freedom-to-do people do
not raise any questions about our freedom to will,
to choose, to decide. It is here, however, where
the control exercised by contingencies of reinforcement enter the picture. The threat of punishment is a good example of control without
physical compulsion. How 'free' are we when we
act under the threat of punishment? According to
Skinner, except for the case of out and out
physical restraint we are least free and dignified

when we are under the threat of punishment. One would expect, then, following Skinner's line of argument, that the literatures of freedom and dignity would attempt to minimize control through threat of punishment. Yet, as we saw the literature of freedom and dignity frequently saves its best shots for control of any sort. This inevitably weakens the fight against aversive control.

What's wrong with controlling behavior by the threat of punishment? First of all, we must distinguish punishment from aversive control. In punishment, aversive stimuli are presented in order to get an organism to stop behaving in a certain way. Aversive control involves the removal of aversive stimuli in order to induce an organism to behave in a certain way. Now the threat of punishment may in some cases itself be an aversive stimulus--when the organism is 'aware' of the threat. We don't like to be punished, but we do not like to live in fear of punishment either. An in-fear-of-punishment situation is itself aversive and can be used either in punishment or in aversive control. Punishment does not merely reduce the likelihood of certain behavior, and stopping punishment does not merely increase the probability of certain behavior; there are serious side effects. The individual seeks to and learns to avoid punishment situations altogether. "Some ways of doing so are maladaptive or neurotic, as in the so-called 'Freudian dynamisms'." (76) Any behavior which results in avoiding punishment will be reinforced. This can include behavior which is harmful to the individual. More effective ways of avoiding punishment include avoiding occasions and situations where punishable behavior is likely to occur, and decreasing the probability that the punishable behavior will occur through modifying emotional and physiological conditions. Skinner's example of these are counting to ten to reduce anger and using a tranquilizer to control aggressiveness. Why not remove the burden of finding ways of avoiding punishment from the shoulders of the individual, by

67

trying to construct a world where this will not be necessary?

> We try to design such a world for those
> who cannot solve the problem of punish-
> ment for themselves, such as babies,
> retardates, or psychotics, and if it
> could be done for everyone, much time
> and energy would be saved. The defenders
> of freedom and dignity object to solv-
> ing the problem of punishment this way.
> Such a world builds only automatic good-
> ness. (62)[39]

There is fear that the environment and not the individual will get credit for good acts. Nobody would need goodness. There would be no room for autonomous man in an all-good environment. Skinner does realize that we are a long way from an all-good environment. For now and for the foreseeable future people must be able to handle aversive situations. The days of automatic good-ness are far off. Doesn't our world--a world in which people cannot be good automatically-- require punishment and aversive control?

> To prepare people for a world in which
> they cannot be good automatically, we
> need appropriate instruction, but that
> does not mean a permanently punitive
> environment, and there is no reason why
> progress toward a world in which people
> may be automatically good should be
> impeded. The problem is to induce
> people not to be good but to behave
> well. (63)

----

[39]Can we really treat each other as babies, retardates, or psychotics? We can't (and shouldn't). And the reasons for this cast doubt upon some of Skinner's more extreme sounding statements. More on this in later sections.

Where threats become less obvious it looks as
if the individual acts have their source in inner
determinations. He exerts self-control, he follows the dictates of his conscience. But what
does conscience dictate and why? For Skinner conscience is simply a messenger for the verbal community. Conscience follows rules formulated by
the verbal community derived from an analysis of
contingencies. (The individual does in some cases
devise his own rules.) Rules are followed either
because they are effective--they provide an analysis of contingencies--or because the verbal community imposes sanctions--sets up contingencies--
e.g., punitive contingencies--which produce the
appropriate rule following behavior. Where the
controlling contingencies--either those expressed
by the rule of those imposed by the community to
get people to follow the rule--are relatively
invisible, we attribute the good behavior to the
goodness of autonomous man.

> Goodness, like other aspects of dignity
> or worth, waxes as visible control
> wanes, and so, of course, does freedom.
> Hence, goodness and freedom tend to be
> associated. John Stuart Mill held that
> the only goodness worthy of the name
> was displayed by a person who behaved
> well although it was possible for him
> to behave badly and that only such a
> person was free. Mill was not in favor
> of closing houses of prostitution; they
> were to remain open so that people could
> achieve freedom and dignity through self-
> control. But the argument is convincing
> only if we neglect the reasons why people
> behave well when it is apparently pos-
> sible for them to behave badly. (my
> emphasis, 66).

When we combine considerations of punitive
control with considerations of merit or desert, we
encounter the concept of responsibility. Just or
fair punishment requires responsibility. Determining responsibility is prominently a legal

69

matter. As such it involves both questions of fact, but also questions which seem to involve the psychology of the inner man. Questions of knowledge, intentions and premeditation appear to commit the law to what Skinner has argued is an outmoded psychology. But appearances can be deceiving. Just as it is not fair to identify the man on the street with the Cartesian dualist simply because he talks about changing his mind or mind over matter, it is not fair to provide mentalistic, theoretical (explanatory) underpinnings to legal talk about intention and premeditation. We can keep to modes of talking if we can provide some accepted theoretical underpinnings. If the talk and the distinctions expressed are important, we should be able to provide a theoretical salvaging operation. Such an operation is very much like what philosophers term explication or rational reconstruction. We show the harmlessness of a certain idiom by translating it into a preferred idiom. A successful translation permits us to eat our cake and have it too. We can use the familiar but problematic idiom because we have an unproblematic idiom backing it up.

All these questions about purposes, feelings, knowledge, and so on can be restated in terms of the environment to which a person has been exposed. What a person 'intends to do' depends upon what he has done in the past and what has then happened. A person does not act because he 'feels angry'; he acts and feels angry for a common reason not specified. Whether he deserves punishment when all these questions are taken into account is a question about probable results: will he, if punished, behave in a different way when similar circumstances again arise? There is a current tendency to substitute controllability for responsibility, and controllability

70

is not so likely to be regarded as a
possession of autonomous man, since
it explicitly alludes to external
conditions. (68)

Skinner above explicates <u>responsibility</u> in terms
of <u>good husbandry</u>. The usual explication is in
terms of autonomous man. Responsibility entails
freedom in the sense of absence of all (external)
control. Except in cases of obvious external
physical compulsion behavior is attributed to the
free autonomous agent who is responsible for it.
Alcoholism and juvenile delinquency are examples;
(although in both cases there has been considerable movement in the other direction, the
alcoholic is now frequently viewed as sick and the
juvenile delinquent as a 'product of his environment'). Skinner emphasizes that the problem of
juvenile delinquency is not to be solved by
increasing the deliquent's sense of responsibility.
He could have added that <u>emphasizing</u> the delinquent's lack of responsibility is no answer
either. The last thing we want is for the delinquent himself to 'give up' on doing something
about his behavior; to say: I'll do what I want--
after all I'm not responsible; it's society and
hang society! Good husbandry demands care in setting up alternatives to punitive contingencies.
Ultimately we need to reform the environment
responsibly. In the short run, we must concentrate on not inadvertently rewarding the undesirable behavior.

Skinner points out that giving credit to
others is frequently a way of escaping one's own
responsibility. This is poignantly illustrated in
some of our educational practices.

The teacher who gives the student credit
for learning can also blame him for not
learning. The parent who gives his child
credit for his achievements can also blame
him for his mistakes. Neither the teacher
nor the parent can be held responsible.(73)

71

To summarize at this point, we may characterize Skinner's views as follows: The literatures of
freedom and dignity are guilty of <u>overkill</u>. In
concentrating upon the escape from aversive situations, they have performed and indeed still perform an important function. They promote the
legitimate goal of freedom from aversive control.
But they have confused aversive control with control of any kind. They have in other words, come
to treat all control as aversive. Because of this
they stand in the way of an effective control of
the human environment--a control which is made
possible today by advances in the (Skinnerian)
science of human behavior. The literatures of
freedom and dignity have outlived their useful-
ness. (This, of course, remains the fundamental
issue.) Effective control is now the pressing
problem. We need to avoid aversive control--but
not so much because it limits freedom--but rather
because aversive control is simply ineffective.
The moral aversion to aversive control can be
replaced by a recognition of the technological
fact that aversive control is poor control. Once
we recognize this we no longer need the literatures of freedom and dignity to safeguard us from
aversive control. The literature of Skinnerian
behaviorism makes progress possible--without
requiring aversive control.

We have seen how punishment and punitive
control play a role in the defense of freedom and
dignity. Acting under the threat of punishment
leaves room for freedom, credit and responsibility.
Threats give a person a chance to act in a manner
which may result in the removal of the threat--
without at the same time physically compelling the
appropriate action. If the appropriate action
resulted from positive reinforcement, then we have
to credit the reinforcers and not the person for
the action. This raises the spectre of automatic
goodness. This is considered to be too high a
price to pay for goodness by the defenders of
autonomous man.

Skinner next takes up alternatives to punitive control. The freedom and dignity people do not employ punitive control exclusively. But any control they do employ must leave the necessary room for autonomous man. Hence, says Skinner, they are limited to weak ineffective measures of control. Skinner first discusses permissiveness. This seems to involve the absence of all control-- really it simply amounts to having no policy of control. "To refuse to control is to leave control not to the person himself, but to other parts of the social and nonsocial environments." (79) Another approach is the maieutic or midwife approach. Basically midwifery involves controlling without appearing to control. The reluctance to admit controlling minimizes the effectiveness of the procedure. Good results must be attributed to something mysterious. In Plato's Meno a slave boy is supposed to have learned some geometry with Socrates serving as midwife. Socrates, however, is supposed to have exerted no control beyond his function as midwife. For instance, Socrates is said not to have really taught the boy anything. Well, if this is the case, where did the learning come from? Who or what exerted the control? Plato's reminiscence theory ultimately traces the control back to a prior state of the boy's soul-- a state in which the soul moved about among the forms of Knowledge. At birth the soul goes through the shock of incarceration and it and the slave boy who is this union of soul and body is said to have forgotten what he previously knew. Midwifery simply helps the boy to remember. Of course, as Skinner points out, there is no evidence that the slave boy really learned anything. But supposing he did, he didn't do it by himself or simply with the aid of Socrates' midwifery. On Plato's account, the control goes back to a certain environment (the World of Forms) which the boy's soul had previously been exposed to.

Other alternatives to punishment discussed are guidance and building dependence on things. The latter is closely tied to the program of progressive education or learning by "Deweying."

73

Dependence on things is sometimes said to characterize independence, but this is not the case.

> Dependency on things is not independence.
> The child who does not need to be told
> that it is time to go to school has come
> under the control of more subtle and
> useful stimuli. The child who has
> learned what to say and how to behave
> in getting along with other people is
> under the control of social contingen-
> cies. People who get along together
> well under the mild contingencies of
> approval and disapproval are controlled
> as effectively as (and in many ways
> more effectively than) the citizens of
> a police state. (86)

Another approach with which we are all familiar is the changing minds approach. Changing
behavior smacks of illegitimate control. Changing
minds through argument and the like, on the other
hand, is not seen as manipulation. After all when
it comes to his mind and what he does with it
autonomous man is in control. It is interesting
that truly effective ways of changing minds or
changing behavior by changing minds are labelled
with the perjoratives "propaganda" or "brainwashing." It is once again a matter of the
obviousness of the controlling variables along
with their effectiveness. Freedom and dignity
require the appearance of incomplete control.
This is something that "brainwashing" and to a
lesser extent propaganda take away from us.

> The illusion that freedom and dignity
> are respected when control appears
> incomplete arises in part from the
> probabilistic nature of operant behav-
> ior. Seldom does any environmental
> condition 'elicit' behavior in the all-
> or-nothing fashion of a reflex; it
> simply makes a bit of behavior more
> likely to occur. A hint will not itself
> suffice to evoke a response, but it adds

74

strength to a weak response which
may then appear. The hint is conspicuous, but the other events
responsible for the appearance of the
response are not. (91)

The general moral to be drawn from the discussion of alternatives to primitive control is
the following: Freedom and dignity seem to
require only weak forms of non-aversive control.
(Aversive control too, it would seem, could not be
so strong as to involve something like physical
compulsion. Skinner writes as if freedom and
dignity require any kind of aversive control but
only weak forms of non-aversive control. Thus it
would seem there is something like an automatic
goodness which can result from very strong punitive measures. For example, being good from
extreme fear or intimidation. Telling the truth
with a gun at your back.) But weak control is
simply inconspicuous and usually ineffective
control.

CHAPTER VI

Values

Skinner's discussion of values is not the strongest chapter of Beyond Freedom and Dignity. This is unfortunate for a number of reasons, not least of which being philosophers will inevitably focus upon a chapter-heading values in the attempt to size up an author's philosophical sophistication. It is not so much that Moral Philosophy has been the field where philosophers have done best, but rather that it has been the field where philosophers have come up with the most ingenious reasons for their not having done well at all. Philosophers recently have concentrated on questions of meaning and reasoning in ethics. These are said to be meta-ethical concerns. Theories have been put forth to the effect that 'good' is the name of unique indefinable, non-natural property, that all ethical judgments are commands or at least involve prescriptions in an important way, that ethical reasoning is a form of reasoning sui generis with its own standards of validity-- standards other than those of logical deduction or induction, for example. Philosophers in short have been busy being subtle in ethics. I think it is fair to say that there does not exist today any consensus as to the meaning of ethical terms or the precise nature of ethical reasoning. There is, however, a consensus on how difficult the problems are and on what a relatively sorry philosophical state ethics is in.

Now, into this well-cultivated chaos comes Skinner and suggests that things are really quite simple after all. The philosopher is suspicious. Value considerations enter Skinner's discussion in the following way. Given that we have a science of human behavior ready for application, how in fact are we to apply it? Who should do the controlling (apply the science) and for what ends?

The answer to these questions seems beyond the reach of science.

> Decisions about the uses of science
> seem to demand a kind of wisdom which
> for some curious reason, scientists
> are denied. If they are to make value
> judgments at all, it is only with the
> wisdom they share with people in general.
> (97)

Skinner says that a behavioral scientist need not accept the charge. This seems to imply that the behavioral scientist can handle questions about ends, about valuation as well as questions about means, about explanation and prediction. It looks as if traditional ethical questions are to be given scientific answers. But the reader should be wary of this interpretation. Traditional ethical questions are after all questions about autonomous man and his decisions freely willed. If ought implies can as most philosophers agree, what is left of ethics if autonomous man goes? (Well, it's a matter of how we construe 'can', etc.) Skinner rejects traditional ethics, so he cannot very well be offering scientific answers to traditional ethical questions. In the chapter on values, he is not playing the traditional ethical game at all. We will raise the important question, as to whether he can avoid playing the game altogether in a later section. In short, the suggestion is that we construe what Skinner is doing in the chapter on values as redefining the questions of traditional ethics so that they become questions about the way people behave--questions about what people value and the conditions under which they value what they do. Explicit judgment about values is to be construed simply as a species of verbal behavior.

That Skinner should be interpreted in the suggested way is supported by the following considerations. Skinner tells us that behavioral scientists can handle questions about ends. Why?

Because "how people feel about facts or what it
means to feel anything, is a question for which a
science of human behavior should have an answer."
(97) But this is hardly the question about ends
with which traditional ethics is concerned.
Skinner proceeds to the question:

> If a scientific analysis can tell us
> how to change behavior, can it tell us
> what changes to make?

He has a ready response.

> This is a question about the behavior
> of those who do in fact propose and
> make changes. People act to improve
> the world and to progress toward a
> better way of life for good reasons,
> and among the reasons are certain
> consequences of their behavior; and
> among these consequences are the things
> people value and call 'good'. (98)

But all this seems to be beside the point. The
man who asks about ends is not asking for an
explanation of anyone's behavior but rather for a
justification of behavior. Was the behavior right
or wrong, good or bad? Not--How did it come about
that the behavior was judged right or wrong, good
or bad? Skinner should have told us, or rather
reminded us, right at the outset that he completely rejects the traditional ethical notion of
justification. The reason is that this notion
implies the scientifically illegitimate notion of
autonomy. It is not really the case that we
are free to choose among alternatives on the basis
of justifications. He pokes fun at the philosopher, Karl Popper, just for this reason. Skinner
had just emphasized that the important thing insofar as values are concerned is to identify the
contingencies that control behavior denominated
good or bad, right or wrong, etc. Given this
information, we can then work towards generating

the valued behavior. Karl Popper has stated a
contrary traditional position as follows:

> In face of the sociological fact that
> most people adopt the norm 'Thou
> shalt not steal,' it is still possible
> to decide to adopt either this norm,
> or its opposite; and it is possible to
> encourage those who have adopted the
> norm to hold fast to it, or to dis-
> courage them, and to persuade them to
> adopt another norm. It is impossible
> to derive a sentence stating a norm or
> a decision from a sentence stating a
> fact; this is only another way of say-
> ing that it is impossible to derive
> norms or decisions from facts. (108)

Skinner's argument can be recast as follows:
We can derive what people will do including what
norms people will adopt, from facts. If this is
so, then to talk about what norms people ought to
adopt is besides the point. What meaning is
there left for "ought?" The sort of "ought" which
cannot be derived from an "is" involves an
illegitimate "can." We are beyond this "can";
hence we are beyond this "ought." Insofar as
value questions are viewed as involving this
"ought" we are beyond them too. As I indicated
above, it is one thing to permit Skinner to inter-
pret value questions as scientific questions for
the purpose of exposition and analysis; this
simply amounts to letting Skinner talk about what
he wants to. It is another thing to grant that we
are beyond traditional value questions alto-
gether--that Skinner and the rest of us can avoid
raising these questions--that we are beyond
ethics. Or to put the matter in somewhat more
Skinnerian terms, will the contingencies ever be
such as to cause us to quit playing the ethical
game altogether?

On the whole, Skinner approaches value questions not as a value-er but rather as a scientist

providing an account of our valuing behavior.
Hence he does not provide us with a method of
handling value questions. He approaches values
from the perspective of an observer rather than
that of a participant. His discussion does not
show that the behavioral scientist can handle ends
just as well as he can handle means. It is rather
the case that he shows us that the science of
human behavior can account for valuing-behavior in
very much the same way it can account for behavior
in general. So it is not true that Skinner provides a scientific way of valuing--He rather
presents a scientific account of valuing. As we
indicated, Skinner could be clearer on the distinction.

Skinner's account deals principally with two
kinds of values or goods--personal values, values
which are the shared inheritance of the species.
This is not exclusively a matter of what the
human organism finds reinforcing or not. Social
values or goods--the good of others--takes us
beyond gratification, towards long-term reinforcers. It is the task of society to temper
this bias by setting up contingencies, e.g.,
establishing maxims or passing laws, under which
the organism is reinforced for passing up short-
term reinforcers in the interest of longer term
reinforcers. Behavior which is reinforcing to
others--social behavior, cooperation--is just the
kind of behavior which the society seeks to
encourage. This behavior will in the long-run be
reinforcing to the individual. Social contingencies are set up with the idea of having everyone
benefiting in the long-run. Skinner speaks of the
justice or fairness of a social environment, and
indicates that it involves a balance between
individualism and its emphasis upon selfish and
short-term goods and to totalitarianism (exploita-
tive systems) with its thoroughgoing emphasis on

the communal and the long-run.[40] People's value-
judging behavior, the appeal to justice and fairness, plays an important role in organizing these
behaviors in general. For Skinner to point this
out does not involve him in making value-
judgments. That he shares with his community certain standards of justice or fairness, that his
value-judging behavior is what it is and not
another thing, is a fact about Skinner, the man,
the member of the community. It need play no role
in his account of valuing and value-judging behavior. Skinner has no particular difficulty with
ends, or with ideals like justice or fairness for
two very different reasons, reasons which he does
not keep sharply enough apart. (i) Skinner need
make no value judgments at all in his scientific
account of value-judgment behavior. When he says
he is going to handle value judgments, he only
means that he is going to fit these into the
framework of the science of human behavior. (ii)
Skinner, the man, as a matter of fact accepts the
basic ends and ideals of the community in which he
is a member. He doesn't really see much problem
with these and is willing to take things like
justice and fairness as given, as it were. Since
there is really no problem here with ends, the
only problem which remains is the technological
one of accomplishing the ends. It is to this task
that Skinner offers his science of human behavior.
In short Skinner presents a causal account of
values. He accepts the basic societal values as
he finds them; and sees the real problem as one of
technology, specifically as a problem of cultural
engineering.

To return to the causal account of values, we
find that personal value and social values are not
together exhaustive of human values. To the good

---

[40]The identification of individualism with
short-term interests is misleading. Most
individuals emphasize prudential or long-term
concerns.

of the individual and the good of others must be
added the good of the culture. (Culture presumably involves practices which go well beyond
social practices. The line between the social and
the cultural is not especially well drawn by
Skinner.) Good for others is not to be identified
simpliciter with good for the culture.

> Presumably there is an optimal state of
> equilibrium in which everyone is
> maximally reinforced. But to say this
> is to introduce another kind of value.
> Why should anyone be concerned with jus-
> tice or fairness, even if these can be
> reduced to good husbandry in the use of
> reinforcers? (my emphasis)

> The question with which we began
> obviously cannot be answered simply by
> pointing to what is personally good or
> what is good for others. There is
> another kind of value to which we must
> now turn.

Note the why question in the above passage. It is
ambiguous. Is Skinner raising a question of jus-
tification--Is he asking for a good reason for
people to be concerned with justice or fairness?
Is he asking for a value judgment? Or is he asking the following question--What are the causal
factors which explain why anyone is as a matter of
fact concerned with justice or fairness? The
reader of Beyond Freedom and Dignity soon finds
out that it is exclusively to the latter question
that Skinner addresses himself.

We may summarize our line of argument at this
point. Skinner claims that questions of values
are in reality questions about reinforcers. But
this is ambiguous. The conventional wisdom is apt
to hold that the question about reinforcers is:
What ought man be reinforced by? (What ought he
value, what is valuable?) But this is hardly the
question about value which Skinner has in mind.

His question is: What are the facts about what
people find reinforcing? The other question
involves autonomous man--and his freedom of
choice. This conception was rejected by Skinner
on scientific grounds. Skinner can give a causal
account of the behavior of people who ask the
valuable or ought question. He can even behave
the same way, himself. But then his behavior too
is subject to the causal explanation.

CHAPTER VII

Skinner on Culture

Chapters seven and eight are the heart of
Beyond Freedom and Dignity. The theme is culture
and its design.

> The social contingencies or the behav-
> iors they generate, are the 'ideas' of
> a culture; the reinforcers that appear
> in the contingencies are its 'values'.
> (121)

Previously we have dealt with two kinds of values
as reinforcers--the personal (which are tied to
the genetic inheritance of the individual organism
and the social which are tied to genetic inheritance not directly but through the mediation of
the behavior of other persons. One has to learn
to act for the sake of another's good. The new
and central value which is at this point introduced is the survival of the culture. Skinner
makes much of the basic analogy between biological
and cultural evolution. The survival of the
culture amounts to the survival of its practices.
New practices correspond to genetic mutations and
survival is the ultimate test for both new
cultural practices and genetic mutations. One
disanalogy between cultural and biological evolution is that the former is Lamarckian--acquired
practices are transmitted.

Skinner recognizes that anyone in the cultural design or engineering business is largely
going to share the values (the reinforcers) of his
culture. He will, of course, be affected by personal goods, and social goods--goods of others--
which are derived from personal reinforcers, as
well as the good or goods of the culture. But how
does the good of the culture become effective?
What makes anyone in general, the cultural
designer in particular, care about the survival of
the culture? Skinner's answer is simple. Concern

for the survival of the culture--or even more
broadly, the <u>humanist</u> concern for the survival of
mankind--is produced by the culture itself. It is
all a matter of whether cultural practices themselves induce members to work for survival. It
is true that much promotion of the culture is
unintentional. But insofar as what might be
termed <u>pure</u> concern for the culture--

> The simple fact is that a culture which
> <u>for any reason</u> induces its members to
> work for its survival, or for the sur-
> vival of some of its practices, is more
> likely to survive. (130)

The culture causes us to be concerned with its
survival. (It had better, for its own good.) But
the question arises as to whether a culture is
<u>worthy</u> or <u>deserving</u> of survival. This is a ques-
tion with which Skinner has some difficulty. Your
culture is supposed to convince you that you
<u>should</u> work for its survival. Effective ways of
accomplishing this would be to convince you that
your culture is at least as good as any alternative or competing culture, i.e., that it deserves
to survive. But we are tempted to ask: Does my
culture really deserve to survive? This kind of
value question or question about ends is not a
legitimate question to the cultural designer. His
task is to design a culture which will meet the
test of survival, on the assumption--culturally
induced assumption--that the culture deserves to
survive. Here again we see Skinner dealing with
questions of ends by <u>simply accepting a set of
given ends</u> or assuming that a culture will provide a set of ends, and taking seriously the
technological problem of how these ends are to be
accomplished. Skinner is mostly concerned with
the means by which a culture can successfully per-
petuate itself. This is an engineering task. The
cultural engineer gets to work only when it is
assumed the culture deserves to survive. The
cultural designer has his task to design a culture
<u>which will</u> survive. The question as to whether

the culture deserves to survive is more than a question of whether the culture is reinforcing to its members. For this would not be sufficient to produce a long range concern with the survival of the culture. Why should I care what happens to the culture after I receive the benefits?

To sum up: How are we to judge the value of a culture?

> Survival is the only value according
> to which a culture is eventually to be
> judged, and any practice that furthers
> survival has survival value by defini-
> tion. (130)

Why should I work for the survival of the culture? The only honest answer to this kind of question seems to be this:

> There is no good reason why you should
> be concerned, but if your culture has
> not convinced you that there is, so much
> the worse for your culture. (130)

Skinner's answer to these questions underline in a dramatic way the extent questions of ends are deemphasized on Skinner's account. There are even problems with the coherence of Skinner's account in this connection. Take the first question: It is difficult to see why <u>survival</u> should be given the prominent place Skinner gives it. Is Skinner claiming that as a matter of fact survival will be the only value by which a culture can be judged? This is a <u>prophecy</u>. Or is he claiming that the cultural engineer can only be concerned about questions of survival, and that <u>his job</u> can only be judged by his success in furthering survival? Skinner cautions his reader against confusing evolution with growth or the later time with the superior. So why should survival prove anything about the value of a culture? But perhaps we are misled by the term <u>value</u> in the question. Per- haps we are taking the term too seriously and Skinner not seriously enough. Values are questions of reinforcement. So we should speak of whether the survival of the culture is reinforcing--but reinforcing to whom? To the members of the culture? But surely the members of the culture will usually not judge the value of their culture now or eventually exclusively upon the criterion of survival. If not to members of the culture then to an outsider, a member of some other culture? But such an outsider will have his own culturally induced values to judge with. Perhaps, it is the behavioral technologist who introduces the significance of survival. But the question of whether the survival of a particular culture is reinforcing is a matter to which technologists are not concerned, qua technologists, but rather a matter which concerns the technologist qua member of a culture. Surely technology does not itself induce an independent concern with survival. The survival of inefficient machines would not be reinforcing, for instance. It is difficult to see that Skinner has any firm ground at all to stand upon when he tells us that "survival is the only value upon which a culture is eventually to be judged."

If there is an answer to the kind of objection we have raised above, we should find it in a chapter labelled "The Design of a Culture" (Ch. 8). The technology which will be employed to effect the cultural design is ethically neutral. It is the matter of design which raises ethical or value considerations. To this point, however, design seems to involve nothing more than design-for-survival. In this chapter too, the emphasis is placed prominently upon workability. The key question is: will it work--will it survive? And this is after all a matter of technology. (Why should workability, any more than survivability, exhaust value?)

In an experiment we are interested in what happens, in designing a culture with whether it will work. This is the difference between science and technology. Utopias, like his own Walden Two and various Walden II type communities which have sprung up from time to time, are viewed as experimental cultures. Here too the key question is--will it work? Historical evidence, Skinner admits, is always against anything new, so we shouldn't be unduly sceptical of Utopian ventures. But what should a workable Utopia be like? What practices should it have? We know at least that the practice must have survival value. But what more? Skinner emphasizes that man <u>can</u> save himself if he applies the available technology. The problem is to get man to apply the technology. Designing a culture is admittedly a terribly ambitious undertaking. Claims have been exaggerated and limitations neglected.

There are basically two objections which critics have offered to the Skinnerian program of cultural reform. The objections neatly complement one another. One argues that the program is impracticable--it can't be done. The other claims that even if the program were practicable, it wouldn't be desirable. As we indicated, Skinner admits the ambitiousness of the program. His conception of utopia or experimental culture gives us some idea about his approach to cultural change. We may reasonably (fruitfully) experiment in a small community or commune with our cultural practices.[41] After all this experiment culture is itself anchored in an ongoing culture that is ready to reassimilate the experimenter if this should become necessary. Imagine the risks on the other hand involved in experimenting with the national or international economy! The risks would, of course, be enormous. Now, Skinner does sometimes speak as if the consequences of not applying behavioral technology would themselves be grave. We are faced with "terrifying problems," he tells us. We could solve these problems by employing a technology of behavior which is now

---

[41]Such experiments are being carried out--in a commune in Virginia, for instance.

available. Freedom and Dignity get in the way.
They interfere with both a proper understanding
of human behavior by positing autonomous man as an
explanatory entity, and with the application of a
genuine science of human behavior by viewing all
control as pernicious. Beyond Freedom and Dignity
(and indeed the corpus of Skinner's work) is an
attempt to sell a number of theses which can put
in order of increasing philosophical cost. First
of all, it is selling Skinnerian psychology. To
buy this, one has to accept Skinnerian psychology
as at least as good as any other approach to the
study of human behavior. The second thesis says
that a science of human behavior can be employed
in modifying human cultural practices for human
betterment. This thesis is ambiguous. Certainly
knowledge is power in some cases. There is a real
question, however, about the proper ratio of
quantity of knowledge to quantity of power in
varying situations. There is for one thing the
old saw about a little knowledge being a dangerous
thing. How much knowledge is enough? How much
knowledge will it take to give us the power we
want? Is Skinnerian psychology ready to undertake
cultural reform? In what areas? On what scale?
The third thesis can be put as follows: Our
attitudes should be adjusted so as to make room
for the application of Skinnerian psychology. (We
must leave freedom and dignity aside in our
attempt to solve our serious problems.) Here too
it is far from clear what we are buying. It is
one thing to be open-minded towards Skinnerian
experimental cultures--Walden Two's--quite
another to permit an experimentation with our form
of government or economy. Skinner is not unaware
of these considerations.

CHAPTER VIII

Morality, Reasons and Causes

Judgments about the effectiveness of institutions are really judgments of applied science, technology or praxiology. They are of the form: Given the purpose of x, on the basis of a scientific examination of x, x is effective (ineffective). These are judgments about the commensurability of means to ends. Skinner rejects the institution of morality. (At the least he suggests radical revisions.) What is substituted will either be a radically different morality, or something so radically different as not to be morality at all. The general end, human happiness, is not disputed. The general characterization of morality as a system of social control remains also. What goes then? The obvious answer is: things like dignity, responsibility, and retributive justice. But this really means that (i) rules or principles explicitly dealing with these notions are to be eliminated (ii) Behavior, linguistic or otherwise, is to be under the control of rules or contingencies which can be stated as rules and which also do not involve the above notions. Speaking loosely, morality is replaced by the applied science of human behavior. Skinner, participating in the theoretical and applied operant psychology institution or practice, examines the practice of morality and finds that we could do better without it. The time is right for an old practice to be replaced by a new one--for morality to give way to science or more accurately applied science.

Contemporary philosophers of social science are likely to have at least two criticisms of Skinner's treatment of morality. (i) A causal account of morality of the kind Skinner offers is in principle incapable of providing an understanding morality. (ii) The judgment that Skinner makes in which he finds morality wanting as an

91

institution is itself inappropriate. (Point two
is not altogether independent of point one.) Let
us look at (i). The objection when spelled out is
likely to go something like this. Morality is an
institution which involves a complex web of various sorts of human conduct. The institution
itself defines what conduct is appropriate upon
what occasions. It states the possible (i.e.,
permissible) moves and provides standards for
judging the appropriateness, or better, the goodness or rightness, of moves. Every good move is,
of course, a permissible one; but not all permissible moves are good ones. Understanding an
institution like morality involves explicating the
rules of the moral game, the rules of moral practice. Understanding any particular bit of moral
behavior involves placing it within the institu-
tional context--showing just how it is permissible
under the rules and showing, if possible, how the
piece of behavior is appropriate to the particular
circumstances. This task might be termed the task
of rationalizing or since this term has been given
a bad name by Freud, intelligibilizing the action.
One shows an action intelligible when one comes up
with a reason for the appropriateness of the
action. The reasons adduced need not have been
'consciously' held by the agent. It is rather the
case that he could recognize these to be good
reasons for what he did, had someone suggested
these reasons to him. (Some writers would not
even insist on this last condition.) The operative word in this criticism of Skinner's in particular and causal accounts of human action in
general is "understand." Understanding an institution and acts falling under it, is to be distinguished from explaining the institution. The
former involves reasons--rationales--the latter
involves causes. Explanation can proceed from
without. The 'explainer' needn't be a participant.
Understanding has to be done from within. The
understander must be a participant in the institution in question or he must be able to imagina-
tively put himself in place of a participant--he
must be able to empathize with participants.

(This contrast in approach to the study of institutions mirrors almost exactly the current debate in the philosophy of history between the covering law or causal people, led by Carl Hempel and the Verstehen (understanding) or reason people led by William Dray.) As the reader has probably surmised the issues run rather deep and probably are at bottom as at least one writer[42] has put it, ideological and political. For our purposes, it will be enough to get some idea of a Skinnerian response to this kind of objection. We will proceed to sketch such a response. This will be to a large extent conjecture since Skinner nowhere takes up this question explicitly.

Skinner would, it seems to me, attempt to break down the sharp line between reasons and causes.[43] It is true that a distinguishing trait of human behavior is that it is frequently rule-governed. Skinner would have to give account of this species of behavior. In fact he has done just this in "An Operant Analysis of Problem Solving" in Contingencies of Reinforcement. The strategy is to bring rules and, through rule-governed behavior, reasons, into the causal-- contingency of reinforcement--analysis. Reasons will be treated as causes of a certain kind. Rule-following behavior is contrasted with contingency-shaped behavior.

> The difference between rule-following
> and contingency-shaped behavior is
> obvious when instances are pretty clearly
> only one or the other. The behavior of
> a baseball outfielder catching a fly ball
> bears certain resemblances to the behav-
> ior of the commander of a ship taking

---

[42]Arnold Kauffman, The Aims of Scientific Inquiry.

[43]He wouldn't be original in attempting this. See D. Davidson, Actions, Reasons and Causes.

part in the recovery of a reentering
satellite. Both move about on a surface in a direction with a speed designed
to bring them, if possible, under a falling object at the moment it reaches the
surface. Both respond to recent stimulation from the position, direction, and
speed of the object, and they both take
into account effects of gravity and fric-
tion. The behavior of the baseball player,
however, has been almost entirely shaped
by contingencies of reinforcement, whereas
the commander is simply obeying rules
derived from the available information
and from analogous situations.[44]

The keystone of Skinner's analysis involves treating rules as discriminative stimuli, contingency-
specifying stimuli, which are constructed to
improve the chances for successful behavior.
Rules play an important role then as controlling
variables. They are a species of S^D.[45] But, and
here is where Skinnerian explanation goes well
beyond understanding, there is more involved in
explaining rule-governed behavior than identifying
rules. A rule is only effective as one among many
contingencies of reinforcement.

After all, why should a man obey a law,
follow a plan, or carry out an intention?
It is not enough to say that men are so
constituted that they automatically follow rules--as nature is said, mistakenly,
to obey the laws of nature. A rule is
simply an object in the environment. Why
should it be important? This is the sort

---

[44]My emphasis. Contingencies of Reinforcement, p. 146.

[45]This assumes the contingencies of reinforcement analysis is adequate for language. See
B. F. Skinner, Verbal Behavior.

> of question which always plagues the
> dualist. Descartes could not explain
> how a thought could move the pineal
> gland and thus affect the material
> body; Adrian acknowledged that he could
> say how a nerve impulse caused a thought.
> How does a rule govern behavior? (148)

Skinner's answer to this question involves, of
course, the contingencies of reinforcement analysis. The effectiveness of rules is explained in S^D
precisely the same way the effectiveness of any
is explained. The reinforcers with which we are
concerned in the moral and political sphere, are
largely social or verbal in Skinner's rather
expansive use of the term. The rules in this case
are likely to express the contingencies which the
society already maintains. To take a step back-
ward for a moment: Can the Skinnerian analysis
provide the sort of understanding recommended by
the reason people? Insofar as this sort of understanding involves simply identifying rule-governed
behavior, this forms a part of the Skinnerian
explanation. Insofar as understanding involves
enumerating reasons, intelligibilization, this
would take the Skinnerian off his main road. But
there is no reason for the Skinnerian to be pre-
judiced against such a detour. He could take it,
if there are convincing reasons for doing so. It
might be the case though that the detour may come
to be a mere distraction. After all, the main
road leads to explanation, prediction and control.
We will eventually want to see just how philosophical travel is to be routed.

     The second objection charges Skinner with
inserting a value judgment where it does not
belong. A causal account of an institution is one
thing, a judgment about the acceptability of an
institution is quite another. No matter how high
you pile the is (descriptive) statements they will
never add up to an ought (prescriptive) statement.
Now in some sense Skinner's judgment that the
institution of morality must (ought to) go, is a
value judgment, and as such it does not belong to

95

the science of human behavior proper. However, judgments about the effectiveness of practices are not thereby removed from the realm of science altogether on Skinner's account. These judgments belong to applied science--to the technology of human behavior. As we saw in discussing education, Skinner makes a great many judgments about the effectiveness of educational practice. But these judgments, though value judgments, are hypothetical or instrumental in nature. Skinner does not dispute the end(s) of traditional educational practice, for instance. The basic end after all is simply to educate. Skinner criticizes the means, the techniques employed to accomplish this end. The criticism is based upon the science of human behavior. The argument is of the form: Given that you want to accomplish such and such, the science of human behavior predicts that the means you have chosen will not have the desired results; or that there are other means which will have the desired and fewer undesirable results than the means you have chosen. When Skinner makes judgments such as these he is standing with one foot as it were in the institution he is criticizing. He adopts the ends of the institution, while the other foot is in the science of human behavior institution. Taking both feet into account, we can say he is standing in the institution of applying science to education or morality, etc. The judgments made are value judgments, but only in the sense of involving some end or purpose of the institution which is under examination. Talk about values appears only in if or hypothetical contexts. If our goal is education, if our goal is human happiness, Skinner can apply his science to make these kinds of value judgments without committing himself to the hypothesized values. He simply rents these values, and applies his science. His job is purely technological. Skinner, however, does more than apply his science in the way we have sketched above. He does accept the ends of education and human happiness (vague phrases). That is to say, Skinner accepts the hypothetical values. This acceptance, though not

96

necessary for technology, does require justification. I see two roads open to Skinner at this point. He can treat these ends as themselves means to more comprehensive ends. These sub-ends become then a matter for technology. He need only "rent" the super-(more comprehensive) ends. He would get these ends by planting one foot within some institution which has the end in question as its primary end. But, of course, we will be tempted to ask Skinner whether he is willing to accept the super-end (whether he is willing to "buy," rather than "rent"). The regress problem is likely to become uncomfortable. Also it is difficult to find super-ends for some ends. Take happiness which we have suggested as the end of morality. As philosophers from Aristotle down have noted, it is hard to conceive a more comprehensive end than this. For Skinner to accept such an end he would have to have both feet squarely planted in the morality institution. He would probably call it the culture institution, and prefer to talk about cultural survival as an end rather than individual or group happiness (or survival). Still accepting a value like survival takes Skinner out of science and applied science and requires a justification independent of these institutions of science taken broadly (to include theory and practice). Skinner is in some sense a moralist in spite of himself. All questions for Skinner are not scientific questions; though it must be emphasized that his criticism of institutions like morality can be viewed as simply technological (praxiological). It is Skinner's involvement as a person, or a participant in the institution of human culture that takes him beyond technology. What takes Skinner then beyond science and technology is the need to justify science and technology as institutions. No particular use of applied science (technology) need require such a justification but the practice as a whole does.

CHAPTER IX

<u>Skinnerian</u> <u>Man</u>: <u>An</u> <u>Appraisal</u>

In the last chapter of BFAD we get back to
the Skinnerian theory of man. Skinnerian man,
Skinner's substitute for autonomous man, is a man
whose behavior depends principally upon two fac-
tors--<u>heredity</u> and <u>history of reinforcement</u>. The
rejection of autonomous man is primarily a rejection of a certain type of psychological theory.
Skinner rejects the appeal to an uncaused cause
or a non-physical cause of behavior. One can it
seems reject Skinnerian man without upholding what
Skinner terms autonomous man. One could appeal to
some factors outside of heredity and history of
reinforcement in explaining human behavior without
appealing to autonomous man as agent, self, soul,
or homunculus. An élan vital theory or a theory
which posits some irreducible chance factor (on
the macroscopic level) would presumably also
reflect a rejection of Skinnerian man. When
Skinner speaks of our being <u>beyond freedom</u>, he
means we are beyond the freedom of autonomous man.
This freedom and autonomous man are inseparable.
Insofar as there are notions of freedom which do
not involve autonomous man, it is far less clear
where Skinner stands. He himself employs freedom
in some contexts, as freedom from (absence of)
aversive control. This <u>freedom from</u>, is not from
aversive control, but from physical coercion is
what many writers have termed <u>liberty</u>. <u>Liberty</u>
is a matter of being able to act without being
physically coerced, or without being under the
threat of physical coercion (initiated by other
men); without being punished or without being
under the threat of punishment. The freedom we
are supposedly beyond is a certain kind of power
to initiate action. But political freedom, or
liberty in the sense employed above does not
<u>prima facie</u> entail any theory of autonomous man at
all. This is, of course, not to say that ultimately there is no connection between the two ideas
of freedom or that our ideas of merit and

punishment do not involve something more than political freedom. One thing we are emphasizing is that there is a close connection between Skinnerian freedom--the absence of aversive control--and political freedom or liberty.[46]

So we see that the fundamental question facing the reader of Beyond Freedom and Dignity is perhaps the following: WHAT CONSEQUENCES--ETHICAL AND POLITICAL--RESULT FROM THE ELIMINATION OF AUTONOMOUS MAN? It seems that the consequences are fewer and less dramatic than the title of Skinner's book would lead us to expect. After all, what we are beyond is simply a certain psychological theory, a theory of the causes of human action--the freedom and autonomous man account of behavior. Essentially we are beyond this because it is bad science. But are we beyond the freedom of the propagandists of political liberty, of the literature of freedom (insofar as the literature of freedom does not smuggle in bad psychology)? Skinner seems to say we are beyond this too. The literature of freedom tends to reject all control (wants to see control of any kind severely limited) where the advocate of Skinnerian freedom is concerned with aversive control. Still there are difficulties here. Skinner identified the advocacy of absence of all control with advocacy of autonomous man--with bad psychology. But on the whole, what the literature of freedom was concerned with was not so much control or causal influence as, coercion. Even in its extreme anarchistic or autarchical statements what was objected to was the initiation of physical force by any man or group of men against the individual. Even this extreme position does not obviously involve the unacceptable psychology of autonomous man.

---

[46]For a penetrating discussion of different concepts of freedom, see F. A. Hayek, The Constitution of Liberty, Chapter I "Liberty and Liberties" University of Chicago Press, 1960.

The literature of freedom plays an important
role in the history of conditioning of western
man. We saw above that this tradition cannot be
rejected simply as either bad psychology or as
involving bad psychology. Well, then should it
be rejected at all? Are we beyond this brand of
freedom too? Skinner's inclination is to respond
in the affirmative, but very little of Beyond
Freedom and Dignity is devoted to confronting this
issue directly (the strategy as previously indicated is the indirect one of linking this kind of
freedom with autonomous man--freedom, and hence
with bad psychology). This literature of freedom
is principally anti-authoritarian, it reflects a
political stance. Skinner thinks this stance is
outdated. The chief threat today he contends is
not from authority or domination, but from the
inefficient use of our resources. We know enough
about human behavior to solve our problems. All
we need is the chance. The we is basically the
Skinnerian psychologists--or behavioral engineers.
The request is for power. Now there seems to me a
great difference between an individual giving the
Skinnerian psychologist the power to treat him for
a problem--a free exchange of services for consideration, and the wholesale transference of
political power to a group of scientists. First
of all the literature of freedom finds little
objection with the former (unless perhaps the
individual contracts away his very life itself--
something inalienable for many exponents of freedom, or libertarians), but with the latter things
are very different. How could a wholesale trans-
fer take place within the bounds of political
freedom? Doesn't this give the authority power
over life and mind? Doesn't this give the authority the right to initiate force on individuals?
Insofar as authority has such power the political
form becomes fascism. Even if a majority should
vote the Skinnerians into power, no majority could
vote the American constitution or more broadly the
fundamental principles of political liberty out of
power. Insofar then as Skinner advocates government by specialists, and the concentration of
political power he stands squarely opposed to the

defenders of political freedom. And he has been duly and frequently taken to task for this. But, and this is of crucial importance to our study, the Skinnerian view of man--the rejection of autonomous man--does not itself entail the rejection of political liberty. Skinnerian man can and <u>in part did</u> live under something like <u>laissez-faire</u> (capitalism) liberalism.[47] There is no reason why Skinnerian behavioral engineering shouldn't be limited to piecemeal application within a libertarian political framework. What must be distinguished are Skinner's personal political preferences, from the political preferences of <u>Skinnerianism</u>. The latter unlike the former has no preferences.

---

[47]Noam Chomsky has called Skinnerian psychology "vacuous" and hence compatible with any political forms, but it is not a matter of vacuity, it is simply a matter of the view of man not <u>entailing</u> any particular political setup whatever. Chomskyan linguistics doesn't <u>entail</u> any specific political form, does it? This is not to say that there aren't associations of ideas or psychological connections.

AFTERWARD

Epistemology Skinnerized

We come finally to the precise relationship
between Skinnerian psychology and philosophy.
This subject should provide a fitting conclusion
for a book entitled "Skinner's Philosophy." We
have seen in some detail how the Skinnerian picture of man compares with some traditional conceptions. Unlike some philosophers, Skinner thinks
we have come a long way in our understanding of
man from the days of Plato and Aristotle. Philosophy of man--philosophical anthropology (psychology)--has been a prominent part of philosophy
since Socrates and his passion for self-knowledge.
Insofar as a great portion of the present work has
been devoted to an examination of the Skinnerian
conception of man, we have already been dealing
with Skinner's philosophy. We have also talked
some about Skinner's theory of science--his philosophy of science, of course.

Still, the central area--the core concern of
philosophy--is and has always been the theory of
knowledge or epistemology. This is the domain
which John Locke in his Essay characterized as
involved with the origin, extent and certainty of
human knowledge or understanding. Locke's
characterization reflects the close connection
between psychology and epistemology. As a historical fact psychology achieved an identity independent of philosophy only in the second half of last
century. Questions of origins or sources--genetic
questions--seem especially appropriate to psychology. But what about questions of extent and
certainly, questions of justification of claims to
know: are these too psychological questions?
There have been a number of attempts to draw the
line sharply between psychology or sociology and
epistemology. Hans Reichenbach in Experience and
Prediction employs a distinction between the context of discovery and the context of justification

to salvage the independence of epistemology from
empirical science. (Reichenbach's distinction,
interestingly enough, mirrors the traditional
Aristotelian/Thomistic distinction between the
order of knowing and the order of demonstration.)
The epistemologist, according to Reichenbach, is
concerned not with actual psychological processes,
but rather with a rational reconstruction of, and
idealized substitute for such processes. The
epistemologist posits an explicit rational or logical substitute for actual psychological processes. The rejection of some story like
Reichenbach's results in the assimilation of epistemology to psychology, or what we could term the
psychologization of epistemology. Skinner does
not face this issue head on; but it is clear that
for him, questions about knowledge are questions
to be answered by his psychology.

This psychologistic attitude is a species of
naturalism with very definite roots in 19th century philosophy. Its chief contemporary advocate
is Skinner's colleague and friend, the Harvard
philosopher, W. V. O. Quine. While Quine's
naturalization of epistemology is more general
than and not wholly consistent with a Skineriza-
tion of epistemology, and examination of Quine's
landmark paper "Epistemology Naturalized" will
serve to place some of these fundamental questions
squarely before us. Whither epistemology? (The
remainder of the present chapter is apt to be
somewhat more technical--more philosophical in a
professional way--than what has preceded. The
issues, however, are clear-cut and fundamental.
Does a large part of philosophy simply collapse
into psychology?)

The theory of knowledge deals with foundations and not superstructures. The philosopher is
concerned principally with a certain aspect of
knowledge or science: he is concerned with the
fundamental terms and principles of science. His
concern is with the starting points of science--
with the privileged terms and principles.

The question is: What sense can be given to foundational investigations? The epistemological enterprise has traditionally been treated as a rebuilding process. We are given a body of doctrine, say Mathematics; and the task is to rebuild it from the ground up on the basis of a firm foundation. Waxing somewhat less figuratively, we can see the epistemological task as involving the selection of a privileged vocabulary, a set of terms we understand very well or exceptionally well, along with a set of privileged truths which (a) are couched in privileged vocabulary (b) are certain, self-evident, reasonable beyond question or possess some such desirable trait and (c) are powerful enough to permit the derivation or generation of all the truths comprising the body of doctrine under examination. In short, the rebuilding process can be looked at as something very much like or perhaps even identical to axiomatization. We axiomatize a given subject matter when we provide a set of basic terms and basic principles (axioms) formulated in these terms from which the truths governing the subject matter can be generated. The paradigm for this sort of rebuilding is Euclid's (albeit inperfect) axiomatization of Geometry. We needn't perhaps identify the rebuilding with the axiomatic style per se since the Cartesian Method of generating all truth on a basis of clear and distinct ideas reflects the traditional picture of the epistemological enterprise just as well. Traditional epistemology, it may be noted, is consistent with both rationalism and empiricism.

As Quine sees it, the axiomatic method must go. Or more accurately, the axiomatic method may remain if we relativize or make a matter of convention the very notion of axiom. There are no axioms, in the sense of self-evident truths in an absolutely privileged vocabulary. There can be no rebuilding from the ground up. There can be nothing but rearranging. The axiomatic style may remain--but only as itself a style of rearranging a given body of truths. Quine sums up the demise of traditional epistemology in the following way:

...I see philosophy not as an a priori propaedeutic or groundwork for science, but as continuous with science. I see philosophy and science as in the same boat--a boat which, to revert to Neurath's figure as I so often do, we can rebuild only at sea while staying afloat in it. There is no external vantage point, no first philosophy. All scientific findings, all scientific conjectures that are at present plausible, are therefore in my view as welcome for use in philosophy as elsewhere.[48]

There is still room for axiomatization per se, but there can be no absolutely first terms and principles. In other words axiomatization remains as a style of rearranging or reorganizing. But it does not follow simply from there being no firsts, that there is no priority, priority, of course, in the sense of prior for certain purposes--even perhaps priority for pedagogical or philosophical purposes. We have cases, usually called reductions, which may be viewed as a kind of axiomatization. Thermodynamics, for instance, can be rendered in the terms of Newtonian mechanics--terms which possess a certain kind of priority--and the theses of thermodynamics can be derived as theorems of Newtonian mechanics.[49] So reduction enterprises make sense even in Neurath's boat. But piecemeal reductions are one thing apparently and the reduction of knowledge, or even empirical knowledge as a whole, is quite another thing. It is reduction on this scale, philosophical or epistemological reduction, if you will, which bites the dust. Why? As the Quine passage

---

[48]W. V. O. Quine, "Natural Kinds," in Ontological Relativity and Other Essays, pp. 126-7.

[49]This is not strictly speaking correct. Additional assumptions are needed for the reduction.

indicated, there is simply no place to the philosopher to stand which will allow him to successfully carry out such a reduction. Let us take the case of empirical knowledge. The philosopher cannot stand within the boat since if he stands within the empirical part of the boat he must assume the subject-matter he is attempting to legitimize through reduction, and if he stands in some non-empirical part of the boat, he is forced to subscribe to some extreme brand of philosophical rationalism which would have empirical knowledge reduced to some non-empirical kind of knowledge. So he cannot stand within the boat. He cannot stand outside the boat because there is literally no place to stand. He drowns. To presume to get out of the boat is among other things to break the continuity between science and philosophy--a continuity which the boat figure expresses.

Well, the nitty-gritty question certainly is: Is it true that we can't get out of the boat? Need epistemology be naturalized? Must questions about justification, evidence, clarity, etc. be replaced by psychological questions? Must all talk of reason be replaced by talk of causes? Prima facie there is something absurd about this. Are we seriously being asked to give up the epistemological enterprise altogether? The question itself (Should we give up the epistemological enterprise altogether?) seems to be something other than a question of psychology. We are fighting an old battle here--the battle of naturalism or scientism. Can one reasonably opt for a justification of science which is not itself scientific explanation or account of science? Do all questions of norms and justification become questions of causes and explanation? These questions are as fundamental as they are difficult to decide without begging questions in every direction. The battle was fought with particular

vengeance in late 19th century German philosophy.[50] Quine's attempt to replace epistemology
with psychology is as we have stated a species of
naturalism--perhaps, the most prominent species--
psychologism. Quine is not especially clear as to
what the psychologization of epistemology involves.
In any event, it seems fair to say that good
psychology replaces good epistemology as a philosophical desideratum; and this result is totally
unacceptable to those philosophers who have in the
past and who still do want to ask epistemological
questions. Psychological understanding is not the
kind of understanding the epistemologist is after.
Perhaps, however, one is forced to give up looking
for this special kind of understanding. Epistemology Naturalized appears to be an extended argument for the above-mentioned result. How good an
argument is it?

Naturalism is not an easy term to pin down.
It seems to come to the view that all questions,
including what have traditionally been considered
philosophical or epistemological questions, are
scientific questions. The problem with this is
the term scientific. Historically, naturalism has
tended to construe science as empirical science.
In this sense Mill's treatment of arithmetic--his
psychologism--is paradigmatic of naturalism in
general. But a naturalist like Quine does not
even recognize a sharp distinction between the
empirical and the rational. We have seen that
for Quine philosophy and science are in the same
boat. One would like to know where if at all
prima facie normative statements are to be found
in the boat. The logical positivists were happy
to toss them overboard. The vocabulary of justification itself is after all a normative one.
Questions of right, of legitimacy, and not questions of fact are at issue. There is little if
any explicit discussion of this kind of question

---

[50]See M. Farber, The Foundation of Pheno-
menology, Chapter I, "The Background of Husserl's
Philosophy."

in Quine. C. I. Lewis had his theory of rational imperatives, Dewey his conception of intelligence and theory of inquiry. We look for something corresponding to these in Quine. Only this will yield a deeper understanding of what is involved in Quine's naturalism.

We come now to the specific argument of Epistemology Naturalized. The epistemological task with which Quine concerns himself is that of providing foundations for empirical knowledge. This task, according to Quine, has two parts: (i) the conceptual task--translating sentences of empirical science into the epistemologically preferred terms of observation (and logic). (ii) the doctrinal task--the derivation of all the truths of empirical science from simple observational truths (and logic). In the words we employed earlier, Quine views the achievement of the epistemological task as the axiomatization of the given subject matter. We have thus: foundations = task of epistemology = conceptual and doctrinal task = axiomatization. It is worth noting that Quine's foundations are exclusively empirical--he views the task of providing foundations as the empiricists have viewed it. He is philosophizing squarely in the Humean tradition. And insofar as the doctrinal task of epistemology (of empirical knowledge) goes, we are still in the "Humean predicament." It can't be done. Things are somewhat more complex with the conceptual task.

Quine identifies the conceptual side of epistemology with rational reconstruction, a favorite philosophical enterprise. There are, or at least were, two good reasons for pursuing rational reconstruction, as Quine sees it:

> One was that such constructions could be expected to elicit and clarify the sensory evidence for science, even if the inferential steps between sensory evidence and scientific doctrine must fall short of certainty. The other

109

reason was that such constructions
would deepen our understanding of discourse about the world, even apart from
questions of evidence; it would make
all cognitive discourse as clear as
observation terms and logic and, I must
regretfully add, set theory.[51]

It is rational reconstruction which bears the
brunt of Quine's criticism. For one thing, how
are we to adjudicate among alternative rational
reconstructions--translations? Still Quine admits
that any such reconstruction would be "a great
achievement." Why? Presumably because of the
"two good reasons" for pursuing rational reconstruction. But at this point Quine drops the
other shoe.

But why all this creative reconstruction,
all this make-believe? The stimulation
of his sensory receptors is all the
evidence anybody has had to go on, ultimately, in arriving at his picture of
the world. Why not just see how this
construction really proceeds? Why not
settle for psychology? [my emphasis]
Such a surrender of the epistemological
burden to psychology is a move that was
disallowed in earlier times as circular
reasoning. If the epistemologist's goal
is validation of the grounds of empirical science, he defeats his purpose by
using psychology or other empirical
science in the validation. However, such
scruples against circularity have little
point once we have stopped dreaming of
deducing science from observations. If
we are out simply to understand the link
between observation and science, we are
well advised to use any available

_____

[51] W. V. O. Quine, Epistemology Naturalized,
pp. 74-75.

information, including that provided
by the very science whose link with
observation we are seeking to understand.[52]

There is substantial philosophical diet in
the above passage. It is the circularity issue
which is preëminent. If we give up the doctrinal
task, Quine tells us, we needn't be afraid of circularity on the conceptual side. Why? Is there
no point of speaking of validation in connection
with the introduction of terms? Does understanding, the sort of understanding the philosopher is
after, amount to nothing but scientific explanation? Of course, the operative world here is
"understanding." Some explication of this term--
some defense of Quine's construction of the term
is required. To ask for an explication of philosophical understanding, however, is to ask for
something very much like characterization of the
philosophical enterprise--the sort of thing philosophers are so reluctant to bother with.

But even if we forget about scruples about
circularity, there is still a good reason for per-
sisting in rational reconstruction. As I see it
this is pretty much Quine's second reason for con-
tinuing the conceptual task even after the
doctrinal task has proven a vain hope. Rational
reconstruction can deepen our understanding of our
discourse about the world. It would be nice if
rational reconstruction could show our physical
concepts to be philosophically legitimate or
innocent "by showing them to be theoretically
indispensible."[53]   Alas this   too proves to be
an impossible dream. Even Rudolf Carnap, whose
Der Logische Aufbau der Welt was the most sus-
tained attempt to carry out this kind of reduction,

---

[52]Epistemology Naturalized, pp. 75-76.

[53]Ibid., p. 76.

threw in the towel by 1936. In "Testability and Meaning"[54] he suggests the method of <u>reduction sentences</u> as a new tool for rational reconstruction. But this marks capitulation insofar as the translational view of rational reconstruction is concerned.

> Reduction forms of Carnap's liberalized kind, on the other hand, do not in general give equivalences; they give implications. They explain a new term, if only partially, by specifying some sentences which are implied by sentences containing the term, and other sentences which imply sentences containing the term.[55]

This new kind of reconstruction does not permit us to eliminate the physical--non-observational terms; and therefore it does not establish the innocence of the former terms. But need <u>legitimization</u> or <u>justification</u> involve such elimination? Presumably for Quine, this is the case. But we search in vain for elaboration or argument on this crucial point.

> The new and more liberal kind of rational reconstruction is a fictitious history in which we imagine our ancestors introducing those (physically addition) terms by a succession rather of reduction forms of the weaker sort.[56]

This is a suggestive characterization; but it no way shows this kind of rational reconstruction to be suspect. The important question concerns the

---

[54]<u>Philosophy</u> of <u>Science</u>, 3 (1936) pp. 419-471; 4 (1937) pp. 1-40.

[55]<u>Epistemology</u> <u>Naturalized</u>, p. 57.

[56]<u>Ibid.</u>, p. 77.

justification of these reduction forms, the justification of the steps in the fictitious history. Furthermore, we can look at rational reconstruction in general as amounting to the creation of a certain kind of fictitious history where we seek reasons for each historical step. But contra Quine, it would seem that the circularity question would obtrude here. For we would not want to assume later historical steps in the attempt to justify earlier steps. Ironically enough Quine himself has made important use of what we might term the method of rational reconstruction as fictitious history, especially in "Identity Ostension and Hypothesis" and "Speaking of Objects." But in these Quine is not explicit about why he spends time with this make believe. However, in Epistemology Naturalized he gives us a reason; but it has little to do with the traditional epistemological motives for rational reconstruction. The new epistemology-naturalized

> could still include, even, something
> like the old rational reconstruction to
> whatever degree such reconstruction is
> practicable; for imaginative construc-
> tions can afford hints of actual psycho-
> logical processes, in much the way that
> mechanical simulations can. But a
> conspicuous difference between old
> epistemology and the epistemological
> enterprise in this new psychological
> setting is that we can now make free use
> of empirical psychology.[57]

So the philosophical world is turned upside down. Rational reconstruction which sought to provide a foundation for science becomes at best a hand-maiden, a helper of science--an aid for the invention of scientific hypotheses.

---

[57]Ibid., p. 83.

For Quine, rational reconstruction provides a definition or it becomes a relic in the philosophical museum. Legitimization = definition; and to

> settle for a kind of reduction that does not eliminate, is to renounce the last remaining advantage that we supposed rational reconstruction to have over straight psychology; namely the advantage of traditional reduction. If all we hope for is a reconstruction that links science to experience in explicit ways short of translation, then it would seem more sensible to settle for psychology. Better to discover how science is in fact developed and learned than to fabricate a fictitious structure to a similar effect.[58]

Quine is asking us to give up a good part of philosophy, is he not? If rational reconstruction goes, then what else is left? One can well sympathize with Quine. There is a profound tendency to disown an especially troublesome child, for instance. Rehabilitation is always an emotionally difficult matter. Traditionally epistemology has been troublesome. Empiricism, rationalism, and in between positions have all shown serious deficiencies. One is apparently left with something of a Hobson's choice insofar as where one is to stand in light of the failure of traditional epistemology to provide firm foundations for science. Scepticism or dogmatism seems all we have left. And perhaps at bottom these two views are not terribly different. Historically, Hume's philosophy can be read as striking a final blow for scepticism, or as showing the necessity for something like animal faith. After all the sceptic does not stop acting; nor does he usually fail to take science seriously.

---

[58]Ibid., p. 78.

Quine's naturalism combines a scepticism in respect to the epistemological task with a dogmatism in respect to science. Science both doesn't possess and doesn't need extra-scientific foundations. The naturalist rather sees himself as presenting a New Deal for philosophy--as making philosophy scientific rather than abrogating it altogether.

We have seen that Epistemology qua foundations of science is an idle dream on Quine's account. In some sense this conclusion is a projection of Quine's evaluation of the epistemology--foundations--of mathematics. I take it that Quine prepares his reader for the relinquishing of epistemology in general by first seeing the necessity of relinquishing it in connection with mathematical knowledge. But the argument in connection with mathematics underlines in a dramatic way the kind of assumption Quine is making throughout. It would take us too far afield to go into detail here, but the following remarks should suffice: (i) Mathematics as a whole is viewed as requiring foundations--even elementary arithmetic. Isn't it more reasonable to view only analysis, let us say, as requiring foundations? (ii) Axiomatic set theory--or more accurately, impredicative axiomatic set theory is taken to be the basis for both the conceptual and the doctrinal task. This gives up the ghost from the beginning, does it not; for as Quine admits this kind of foundation is more in need of foundation than the mathematics which is supposed to be built upon it. Furthermore, the very employment of the Axiomatic method makes possible considerations like incompleteness with further vitiates this kind of foundational effect. Of course, several absolutely central questions come to mind at this point. Why construe the foundational enterprise in mathematics as Quine does? Is there some alternative approach which might serve as a more effective approach to foundational problems in general? Insofar as the former question is concerned, there certainly is historical precedent

for Quine's treatment. He simply identifies the
epistemology of mathematics with the logicist
program--the attempt to reduce mathematics to
logic--actually logic plus set theory. But, of
course, historical precedent is no justification.
There is an important alternative approach--an
approach which may be termed the constructive
approach. This approach has roots in the work of
Brouwer, Weyl, and Heidegger; but it is chiefly
Paul Lorenzen who has developed it into a viable
systematic philosophical alternative. Lorenzen's
program for the theory of knowledge mirrors the
program for constructive mathematics.

The task of philosophy or theory of knowledge
is to construct a language which will be adequate
for theoretical and practical science. This construction, in order to deserve the appellation
critical (or constructive) must not make use of
any uncritically accepted linguistic apparatus.
There are to be no circles and, of course, no
leaps--no steps left out. But how is such an
ambitious program to be carried out? For one
thing we must be able to get out of the boat.
Where do we begin? We begin with human life,
primitive human life if you will. Activities like
hunting and building will be going on, but there
will be an absolute minimum of linguistic activity. Grunts and groans, maybe, but no language as
we know it. Primitive existence might be likened
to the sort of existence people would have float-
ing along on small rafts or logs. Life is primitive because there is no boat available at this
point. The boat must be constructed; and, of
course, all the while life goes on. The philosopher must put himself in the place of these
primitive people, and construct a language which
will unlike the language that developed in the
factual history of the race be a truly rational or
philosophically adequate language. Of course, at
the primitive level there is no full blown notion
of rationality--but there is something like workability or practicability. And it is this notion
which is involved in the first steps of out construction. Explicit or implicit norms which

116

arise at a stage n the construction cannot be
appealed to in justifying some constructions at a
step prior to n. To allow this kind of justification would involve us in circularity. The
reader should be able to see how constructive
mathematics--constructing the mathematical lan-
guage--is literally the model for the constructive
enterprise in general.

Here we can give little more than a sketch or
outline of the constructivist program.[59] The
lowest rung in the linguistic ladder is reserved
for commands or requests--what are in Skinner's
vocabulary labelled 'mands'. Then come action
sentences the introduction of action terms or
action predicates like runs, hits, etc. and proper
names or singular terms in general. All this
greatly facilitates social intercourse, it permits
hunting and fishing, let us say, to be carried out
much more effectively. We are constructing the
boat plank by plank. We have at this point the
various types of simple,--i.e., non-compounded
sentences and we have these to the extent that it
is made clear what is involved in defending and
attacking such sentences. We come to the point
where we must have rules for determining defen-
sibility of compound sentences in terms of the
simple sentences which compose them. These rules
are the rules of logic, and they amount principally to reasonable conventions governing the use
of logical functors or connectors. Logic is
introduced without the aid of fancy philosophical
(semantic) notions like truth and satisfaction; or
metaphysical principles characterizing being-in-
general or reality. There are two reasons for
this: (1) It is not clear that these semantic or
ontological principles can themselves be justi-
fied, (ii) notions like truth, satisfaction and

_____

[59]See Paul Lorenzen and Oswald Schwemmer,
Konstructive Logik, Ethik und Wissenschaftslehre.
See also my own "Epistemology De-naturalized"(Kant-
Studien) 78 for details.

being have not yet themselves been introduced.
Hence to employ these principles for justifi-
catory purposes would involve us in circularity.

Once we have a vocabulary for logic we can
turn to the material sciences. We need basically
a vocabulary for mathematics--the lower and higher
arithmetic. The word 'need' is operative because
we need as much science as would allow us to
prosper technologically. Beautiful theories,
theory for theory's sake, we do not need. Aesthe-
tic notions like elegance, and simplicity, have
after all not yet been introduced. By this stage
the reader will no doubt note that our boat has
come a long way. Life is far from primitive.
Once we have the lower and higher arithmetic, we
need a language adequate to the experimental
laboratory. We have to build instruments and
employ these instruments to make measurements.
Here is where geometry and fundamental or proto-
physics enter the picture.[60] Well this is indeed
very sketchy, but this should give the reader some
idea of what the constructive alternative to
epistemology-naturalized might look like. After
all, it does little good to criticize unless one
has a 'superior' alternative in mind.

I would like to conclude by showing where
Ethics and practical philosophy fit in the constructivist program. The task of philosophy is to
build a language adequate to both theoretical and
practical science. Our boat will then be far more
spacious than Neurath's or Quine's, where normative matters seems to be ignorned altogether.

Where does ethics enter the picture? Broadly
speaking ethical or normative considerations are
present from the earliest steps in our critical or
constructive fictitious history. In building our
language from the ground up each step had to be

---

[60]See for details, P. Janisch, Die Proto-
physic der Zeit, Mannheim.

resonable or justifiable. We worked at this
stage with an implicit criterion of practicability,
but even here practicability recognized or
involved some common interest,...Justification
from the outset involved something more than
individual whim and caprice. On the other hand,
though decisions, the choice of various linguistic conventions, proceeded in accordance with
action principles, it did not proceed by appeal
to these principles for these principles would
themselves have to be formulated. Such principles would come to be formulated when reflection
became necessary when situations arose where
agreement could not be attained within an implicit
frame of justification. We proceed in accordance
with certain principles of justification until the
procedure itself is called into question. Then it
becomes necessary to formulate, to make explicit
the principles, in accordance with which we have
been acting. It is not too difficult to see that
the basic ethical principle will have some thing
to do with objectivity--or the elimination of bias
and arbitrariness; for the entire constructive
procedure, the step-by-step non-circular chain of
justification requires at least implicit recognition of action in accordance with this principle
right from the beginning. The principle of
principles then can be termed the principle of
objectivity.[61] Our critical fictitious history is
then also a normative history. Rational reconstruction, epistemology, is also a normative historical enterprise. The argument for the naturalization of epistemology certainly has not been
made. Psychology, even Skinnerian psychology,
cannot substitute for some kind of first philosophy or epistemology. Skinnerian answers are just
not appropriate to fundamental epistemological
questions. Philosophy and politics as normative

---

[61]See Paul Lorenzen, Normative Logic and
Ethics, for a more detailed discussion of objectivity.

disciplines resist Skinnerian treatment. Our position then is once again that there is no need to stretch a good thing too far.

BIBLIOGRAPHY (Selected)

Chomsky, N. "Review of Skinner's Verbal Behavior." Language, 1959.

Dewey, John. Human Nature and Conduct. New York: The Modern Library, 1930.

Dewey, John. "On the Reflex Arc Concept in Psychology." Psychological Review, 1896.

Hill, W. F. "Learning: A Survey of Psychological Interpretations." New York: Crowell, 1977.

Hook, Sidney. Language and Philosophy. New York: New York University Press, 1969.

Quine, W. V. O. Ontological Relativity. New York: Columbia University Press, 1969.

Russell, Bertrand. Outline of Philosophy. Meridian Books, 1960.

Skinner, B. F. About Behaviorism. New York: Random House, 1974.

Skinner, B. F. Beyond Freedom and Dignity. New York: Bantam/Vintage Books, 1972.

Skinner, B. F. Contingencies of Reinforcement. Englewood Cliffs: Appleton-Century-Crofts, 1969.

Skinner, B. F. Cumulative Record. Englewood Cliffs: Appleton-Century-Crofts, 1972.

Skinner, B. F. Science and Human Behavior. New York: New York Free Press, 1965.

Skinner, B. F. Technology of Teaching. Englewood Cliffs: Appleton-Century-Crofts, 1968.

Thorndike, E. L. The Elements of Psychology, 1913.

Tolman, E. C. Purposive Behavior in Animals and Man. Englewood Cliffs: Appleton-Century-Crofts, 1967.

Watson, John B. Behaviorism. New York: W. W. Norton, 1970.